No Frontier to Learning

by RALPH L. BEALS and NORMAN D. HUMPHREY

No Frontier to Learning

THE MEXICAN STUDENT IN THE UNITED STATES

ASSISTED BY RALPH ARELLANO, AGNES BABCOCK, AND LOUIS STONE

UNIVERSITY OF MINNESOTA PRESS, Minneapolis

Foreword

VISITORS in foreign lands have always been agents of cultural contact and transmission. The increase in "exchange of persons," especially after World War II, has stimulated interest in the mechanisms and consequences of exchange, particularly in the United States where for several years the number of foreign students enrolled in institutions of higher education has exceeded 30,000. Also characteristic of the recent period has been the growth of organized programs of exchange supported by governments, foundations, and other organizations. Since such sponsored exchange has been undertaken with a variety of avowed objectives — ranging from the promotion of international friendship and understanding to the transmission of skills essential to programs of technical assistance and national development — questions have been raised about the effectiveness with which student exchanges have served these purposes. The need for evaluation of programs has been widely recognized, and several major attempts at evaluation have recently been undertaken. To provide adequate guidance for the improvement of programs, however, evaluation must be founded on an understanding of the determinants of effects on the foreign student. Such understanding has been insufficient because of the lack of substantial previous research on cross-cultural education.

In this setting the Social Science Research Council early in 1952 appointed a Committee on Cross-Cultural Education. In view of the divergence among specific aims of programs, and the dearth of empirical knowledge of the processes and effects of exchange, the role of this committee was considered to be distinct from program evaluation; the committee was to plan and stimulate research that might lead to better understanding of the complex process involved in cross-cultural education. Practical considerations led to concentration on present and former foreign students in United States universities. With this narrower focus, the committee hoped to select significant problems and to carry research on them far enough to establish provisional findings and to indicate promising areas for further examination.

Support for a three-year program with this purpose was granted to the council by the Carnegie Corporation of New York, the Ford Foundation, and the Rockefeller Foundation. The present monograph is one of several reports based on research in this program.

The principal studies sponsored by the committee fall into two groups. On the assumption that difference in cultural background is an important factor in determining the consequences of foreign educational experience, intensive studies of students from several countries of contrasting cultures were first undertaken, beginning in the fall of 1952. These studies relied primarily but not exclusively on prolonged personal interviews, and were particularly concerned with the relation of cultural background to the student's adjustment in the United States, and to his readjustment after return to his home country. Four studies in American universities were coordinated by M. Brewster Smith of the council staff. Complementary studies of returned students in their home countries were directed by Cora DuBois, then of the Institute of International Education. All these studies benefited from consultation with John Useem and Ruth Hill Useem, who were then about to undertake for the Hazen Foundation the research reported in their book *The Western-Educated Man in India* (New York: The Dryden Press, 1955). The committee is grateful to them and to the Hazen Foundation for their willing and close cooperation with its efforts.

The second phase of the program comprised more systematic studies of problems and hypotheses identified in the committee's review of findings in the earlier series. Only a few of many challenging leads could be pursued in the second group of studies, carried on during 1954–55. Several apparently important determinants of differing outcomes of sojourn in the United States, particularly determinants of attitudes, were investigated in detail. Mutual relevance of the several projects was again encouraged by joint planning and by frequent communication among the project directors, under the general coordination of M. Brewster Smith.

The foregoing account may well suggest certain cautions to readers of the monographs based on the committee's studies. The early projects focused on nationality groups do give, as intended, a picture of some varieties of experience of foreign students. The small numbers of students that could be interviewed, however, and the lack of systematic sampling mean that generalizations about the frequency of different reactions and their determinants can be misleading. Arbitrary extension of conclusions to all foreign students or to foreign students in a particular situation would be most hazardous. A different reservation is in order with respect to the second group of studies. These were designed to throw light on particular relationships that seemed to be important in the outcome of study in the United States. But focusing on these relationships entailed the neglect of others perhaps equally important. Cross-cultural research, moreover, is still in the pioneering stage. Other compromises and limitations are made explicit by the authors of the respective monographs.

The research sponsored by the committee, it should be emphasized, was not designed to evaluate present exchange programs. Studies of a quite different sort would be required for that purpose. But the monographs inevitably call attention to difficulties and even individual "failures," in their exploration of processes and determinants of adjustment, learning, and attitude formation in cross-cultural experience. A hasty reader, especially if he measures success in terms of complete acceptance of the United States by visitors, may conclude that foreign student exchange is of questionable value. The committee's studies justify no such conclusion. It is hoped that administrators will find in the committee's work a basis for better understanding of cross-cultural education, for more informative efforts at evaluation, and for future decisions as to policy.

The dynamic leadership and wide-ranging interests of Wendell C. Bennett, the first chairman of the committee, played an important part in shaping its task. Both professionally and personally the committee suffered a great loss on his death in September 1953.

RALPH L. BEALS
Chairman, Committee on
Cross-Cultural Education

Preface

THE belief that learning should have no frontiers is deeply embedded in the history of the academic culture of the whole Western world. Nevertheless the phrase "no frontiers to learning" has special relevance to the study of the Mexican students who have attended United States universities and colleges. The contiguity of the United States and Mexico and the permeability of their long common frontier to the flow of scholars and students in both directions has unique effects upon the experiences of Mexican students in this country.

In spite of these factors favorable to exchange, anti-intellectual and hyper-nationalistic groups in both countries tend to view the exchange of students with suspicion. It was in this context that General Lázaro Cárdenas, former president of the United States of Mexico, replying to the head of a national student federation in Mexico who expressed concern over the dangers of undesirable foreign influence resulting from study abroad wrote: ". . . the wish to learn has no frontiers, nor is the desire for truth and justice limited in time or space. On the contrary, it would seem advisable . . . while duly protecting the legitimate objectives of scientific, nationalist and progressive education against illogical intrusion or imitation . . . to use to advantage the investigation, knowledge and experience of modern technique, whatever country it may be coming from." [1]

Unique situational and cultural factors account for some of the differences in this report from other national studies in the program of the Committee on Cross-Cultural Education described in the Foreword. In addition, the Mexican studies were influenced by the anthropological background and biases of the principal investigators.

[1] Quoted from an editorial in *Mexico This Month*, 1:5–6 (May 1955).

ix

Not only were the 1177 Mexican students reported to be in the United States in 1952–53 widely scattered through American universities and colleges rather than clustered in a few institutions,[2] but a substantial number proved to be European quota immigrants who happened to have come to this country by way of Mexico. Moreover, most Mexican students were found to spend several years in the United States and often to study in two or more institutions. Consequently it was impossible to find an adequate number of students at one institution or to focus attention on selected students with comparable experience in the United States.

The part of this study concerned with Mexican students in the United States — the domestic study — is based upon open-ended interviews with Mexican students on the campus of the University of California at Los Angeles and upon written materials supplied both by these students and others located on the campuses of several other United States universities. The interviews and the preliminary analysis of their content were carried out by Ralph Arellano and Louis Stone. Analysis of the written materials was done by Agnes Babcock. The part of this study conducted in Mexico is based upon interviews with returned students in Mexico City and Guadalajara carried on by Norman D. Humphrey. Details concerning the subjects of the study, the nature of the sampling problem, the methods and problems of interviewing, the character of the written materials, and the methods of analysis are presented in Chapter II and in the Appendix. The reader not interested in technical details should be warned that, because of sampling and interview difficulties, the conclusions of this study are not definitive although we believe them to be substantially correct.

Norman Humphrey suffered a prolonged and severe illness following his return from Mexico, terminating with his death in October 1955. As a result he was unable to complete his analysis of his interview materials, many of which remained in his field notebooks. The senior author has made use of the notebooks but has relied mainly for the study of returned students on an article, "The Mexican Image of Americans," [3] and on an unpublished report for the Committee on Cross-Cultural Education.

This monograph was written by the senior author but many of the opinions and conclusions were shared in correspondence and confer-

[2] *Education for One World: Annual Census of Foreign Students in Institutions of Higher Education in the United States, 1952–1953* (Washington, D.C.: Institute of International Education, 1953).

[3] *Annals of the Academy of Political and Social Science,* 295:116–25 (September 1954).

ences and rest in part on Dr. Humphrey's materials. The general plan of a joint monograph had been agreed upon by the two authors. Dr. Humphrey read and constructively criticized an early version of the portion of Chapter I dealing with Mexican culture, and the description of the Mexican educational system is mainly his. Although Chapter 2, "The Mexican Student at Home," is based primarily upon interviews with students in the United States, Dr. Humphrey's notebooks contain a great deal of confirmatory material. Much the same is true of Chapters 3 and 4. Chapter 5 on the returned student draws very heavily upon Dr. Humphrey's material and a substantial part is taken either directly or with slight rewriting or rearrangement from his reports. Nevertheless, since Dr. Humphrey did not see a final version of the manuscript before his death, responsibility for all statements must rest upon the senior author.

The debt that the staff of the Mexican student project owes to the Committee on Cross-Cultural Education of the Social Science Research Council, and the supporting foundations, is obvious. We wish also to express our appreciation to Dr. Clifford Prator, foreign student advisor of the University of California at Los Angeles, and his staff, and to a number of members of the faculty, who advised us or gave information about students. We also wish to express our deep appreciation to those people who made it possible for us to obtain additional background and other written materials from Mexican students at other institutions, especially John W. Bennett, Ohio State University; Richard Lambert, University of Pennsylvania; William H. Sewell and Oluf Davidsen, University of Wisconsin; Ivan M. Ponedel, University of California at Berkeley; James L. Wyatt, Louisiana State University; Dorothy Zeck and Priscilla Ewing, University of Southern California; Ake Sandler, Los Angeles State College; and Byron Holmes, Los Angeles City College. Many others at various institutions too numerous to mention furnished information or attempted unsuccessfully to secure data for us. The staff of the Department of Anthropology and Sociology and the administration of the University of California at Los Angeles cooperated in many ways. Martin Beckman, Charles C. Cumberland, George M. Foster, Olen E. Leonard, and Charles Loomis gave detailed criticisms of an earlier draft of the manuscript. To them all we are grateful.

Above all we are obligated to the many present and former Mexican students who spent so many hours providing the data for this report.

R. L. B.

Contents

No Frontier to Learning

The Cultural Approach

FOREIGN students provide a challenging array of research problems whose solution requires a variety of approaches and the use of tools from all the social sciences. One focus may be on the individual and the influence of his personality and other psychological characteristics on his experience as a foreign student, both while abroad and after he returns, as well as upon the modifications induced in him by the experience. A second approach is situational, examining the effect of different situations on the way the foreign student adjusts, receives, and assimilates new experience while abroad, or reinterprets or utilizes this experience when he returns home. A third possible focus of attention is on the social structure from which the student emerges, the structure of his social relationships during his visit in the host country, and the influence of the social structure on the adjustment of the student after he returns home. Yet another approach concerns itself primarily with the influence and interaction of normative and behavioral patterns at various points in the contact situation.

Such a division of approaches is of course artificial and incomplete. Few social science problems can be exclusively assigned to one or another approach. It is perhaps a virtue of foreign student studies that they emphasize the interdependence of these approaches; to the extent that only one is used, the study will be inadequate. On the other hand, few investigators are equally well equipped to handle all possible approaches, and resources rarely permit the assembly of a team able to follow fully holistic procedures. The various studies prepared for the Cross-Cultural Education project, all use a variety of approaches but each tends to emphasize or focus upon one approach more than another.

This study attempts to make the cultural approach central, viewing

3

social structure as an aspect of culture. In part this choice reflects the background and experience of the principal investigators; in part it is a deliberate attempt to experiment with an approach differing in emphasis from the others. At the same time any complete divorcement of the cultural from the other approaches would be as impossible as it would be undesirable. Yet experience with the Mexican project suggests great caution in using psychological concepts cross-culturally. Although psychological processes undoubtedly transcend cultural lines, they may be equated only at a high level of abstraction; in their behavioral expression they are heavily weighted by cultural experience, and any simple comparison may be woefully misleading. For example, the denial by Mexican males of any conflict situations with their mothers reflects a cultural condition rather than a clinically interesting repression.

In our view the individual and social-psychological processes are set in a matrix of functionally related social institutions and cultural norms which give form and meaning to experience and to behavior. When individuals move into a different matrix, the perception of form and meaning and the appropriate responses to stimulus situations will be enhanced, limited, or directed by the original socio-cultural matrix of the subject. Such terms as "adjustment" hence become very elusive in their meaning, which may differ enormously depending upon the cultural frame of reference of observer and subject. We propose, then, to emphasize culture contact phenomena in our analysis.

Contact between cultures has long been recognized as a major factor in their change and growth and has been a major concern of many anthropologists since the beginning of the discipline. Contacts between cultures vary both in intensity and duration, and of late years most anthropological interest has centered upon acculturation situations, that is, situations where two cultures are in prolonged and close contact with resulting rapid and extensive modifications in one or both cultures. Despite the fact that, in the last analysis, culture exists in and is transmitted by the individual members of a society, in most acculturative situations so many persons are involved that it is possible for many purposes to ignore the individual. Attention rather is focused upon the changes in technologies, institutions, customs, beliefs, value systems, and interactive patterns. Put another way, generalized changes in behavioral patterns may be studied without taking into account the impact of these changes upon the individual or the individual's role in bringing such changes about. In part this is possible because a very large proportion of the individuals in each culture is directly involved in the process; in effect, there is an approach to a total impact of each culture upon the other.

In other cases, contact is much less massive and direct. Especially where cultures lie at a distance from one another spatially, the agents of contact may be a minority of individuals from one or both cultures who may or may not be representative of the total range of the culture or of the society. In such circumstances, knowledge of the individuals concerned is more necessary for understanding of the contact phenomena, especially if the social structure is complex and the culture heterogeneous. In many instances, the agents may be government officials, traders, or missionaries, or some combination of these. Such agents may be drawn from only one part of the social structure and bear with them only selected segments of their culture. They often will exercise influence primarily within selected segments of the host culture and social structure. In such cases knowledge both of the kinds of individuals involved and of their position within the cultural totality becomes important.

The foreign student presents an even more involved form of contact, especially where complex cultures are concerned. In this case the students come from distinctive social positions with correlated cultural backgrounds. The preconceptions with which the student comes, the way he perceives his experience in the host country, and the selective way he absorbs or rejects aspects of the host culture will all be conditioned by his social position, his cultural orientations, and by his individual personal characteristics.

The foreign student, moreover, does not come into contact with the total society and culture of the host country. He enters a specialized situation, the university or college community, located in a limited region of the host country. Circumstances, his personal interests, his exposure to the mass media, his opportunities for observation, and the nature of his personal contacts in large measure determine how thorough his knowledge of the host country becomes and what he takes home on his return. Finally, the influence the foreign student may have on his return home will again depend upon his social and cultural position, a position which may or may not be the same as that which he left to come to the United States. Thus whether the student returns with little more than some new technical skills or with a broad knowledge of the host culture, his direct and immediate impact will be upon a restricted segment of the home culture.

It is, then, not enough to understand the individuals involved in student exchange; it is necessary to understand the situation, the cultures, and the social structures. Personal, situational, social, and cultural factors interpenetrate every problem. To employ a single approach in a study such as this is primarily a matter of the investigator's skills and interests, of methodological convenience — and perhaps also a confession of inadequacy.

Consideration of both individual and cultural approaches is especially appropriate in studying the Mexican student in the United States, for contact between the two cultures approaches the massive type of acculturation. Not only are Mexico and the United States close together, but the boundary is highly permeable in either direction. Each year several hundred thousand North American tourists visit Mexico, supplemented by a smaller but substantial number of businessmen, missionaries, scholars, and students who spend longer periods in Mexico. And a similar but even larger flow occurs from Mexico to the United States. The mass movement from Mexico, however, does not come from the middle and upper class, as does the movement from the United States, but is composed primarily of lower class rural villagers or urban proletarian groups which provide very few of the Mexican students in the United States. And as Mexico is a country of pronounced regional and class differences in culture, differences accentuated by revolutionary changes over the past forty years, understanding the complexities of Mexican culture and society is essential to understanding the Mexican student.

While it is true that the Mexican students are a highly selected group and that certain regions, social groups, and aspects of Mexican culture are unrepresented, the backgrounds of various students are far from uniform. The students are scattered widely through the United States and have undergone substantially different experiences over varying periods of time. As a result the contact situation at the individual level is difficult to identify and control. The diffuseness of the individual contact situations, then, creates methodological difficulties which also encourage new attempts to deal with the contact phenomena at the more abstract cultural level. Material on individuals involved in the study will be presented, but it will be given in a cultural context and be illustrative rather than representative. Thus, the study of the Mexican students emphasizes the cross-cultural problem rather than the individual problem, although these are recognized as being interrelated.

6

At the outset several general questions were posed in dual form by the investigators. At the individual level we asked these questions: (1) What was the Mexican student like before he came to the United States? (2) What happened to the Mexican student during his period of study in the United States? (3) In what ways do the Mexican student's experiences in the United States affect his life on his return to Mexico? The cultural phrasing of these questions is (1) What are the formative socio-cultural influences on the Mexican student before he comes to the United States? (2) What aspects of American culture influence the Mexican student in the United States, and what are their effects? (3) To what extent is United States culture taken back to Mexico, and to what extent does it continue to affect individual behavior or contribute to culture change?

In addition we asked what factors in Mexican culture lead to rejection or acceptance of United States culture or to individual conflict situations. Thus, while concern with problems of individual adjustment is inherent in many aspects of the case-history approach utilized, interest is not focused upon adjustment in the psychological sense, but rather upon the influence of cultural factors on the way the Mexican student in the United States becomes related to an alien physical and cultural environment. Space and time dimensions are considered important in the understanding of these processes, which either change or reinforce the attitudes, values, ideologies, and behavior of the Mexican student. Put another way, the knowledge the Mexican student acquires in the United States, the way he organizes it, and the consequences upon his return are deeply affected by his experience with and perceptions of United States culture, and by his family, class, and cultural background in Mexico. Both of these are mediated by the distinctive personality characteristics of the individual, but only in part have we been able to understand these mediating characteristics across the barrier of the cultural difference between investigator and subject.

The study suggests that the Mexican student differs significantly from students from other cultures; it is probable that he is significantly different from most other Latin American students. A prolonged period of social and economic change in Mexico, coupled with a more mature nationalism, is associated with individual seriousness of purpose, strength of motivation, and self-confidence. Greater knowledge of the United States and its culture permits easier social and personal adjustments while the student is here; failures in adjustment, while perhaps aggravated by the student's

7

situation in the United States, in most cases have their origin in conflicts lying in the individual's Mexican past.

Feelings of hostility toward the United States are not generalized against all Americans — a result of the Mexican version of individualism. Hostility stems primarily from historical events and resentment of the inevitable subordination of Mexico's foreign relations to the power and proximity of the United States. This resentment is expressed, as by students from other countries, in probing at weak spots in our culture, particularly where our practice is contrary to our expressed ideal. On the other hand, Mexicans' sensitivity to criticism of their home country is less than is the case with some other foreign student groups, and centers primarily on foreigners' failure to recognize Mexico's social, political, and economic progress.

The relatively less sensitive reaction of the Mexican to criticism also stems in part from a conscious sense of superiority in many aspects of his culture. The Mexican concedes the United States' great technological superiority, greater order, and more effective political democracy, but he perceives a more profound gulf between Mexican and American culture than is perceived by most Americans. Whether he is religious or not, the Mexican student rejects American "materialism" and is convinced that Mexican culture offers a deeper meaning to human existence and provides a more satisfactory pattern of social relationships.

When we tested the Mexican students on their personal beliefs and ideologies, they indicated that, except for these sensitive areas, they believed themselves to differ considerably from the majority of their countrymen. A group of American students tested on the same items showed a similar divergence from what they believed to be the most common American ideology. Indeed, most of the aspects of American ideology rejected by the Mexican students were even more strongly rejected by the American students. The differences between the average scores of Mexican and American students on a beliefs and ideology test proved less than the differences within each group from its estimate of the ideology of the majority of fellow nationals. For example, Mexicans tend to accept and approve of many aspects of United States government and business. Although the Mexican student continues to feel the family is important, he rejects many traditional attitudes and approves of greater freedom for women, less authoritarian child training, and a broader concept of social relationships. Even though he continues to be more authoritarian in his concepts of personal and social relationships than are most American students, he becomes markedly less authoritarian than seems true of most of his countrymen. Although he remains much more concerned with status symbols than is his American counterpart, he nevertheless rejects the symbols verbally and becomes less status-conscious in behavior.

On the other hand, the American student rejects chauvinistic aspects of American nationalism and American materialism even more strongly than the Mexican student does. And in areas where the Mexican student's ideology tends toward American norms, the American student tends to move away from the American norms toward a common ground with the Mexican student. Within the areas tested, it appears that Mexican and American students tend to share a common ideology which for both groups is significantly different from the way they perceive the prevalent ideologies of their respective countries. Moreover, many of the beliefs and ideologies appear to persist after Mexican students return home and in some measure are reflected in their behavior.

THE NATURE OF MEXICAN CULTURE

Adoption of a cultural frame of reference for the study of the Mexican student compels consideration of the characteristics of Mexican culture. Despite the considerable body of anthropological literature on Mexico, there are few general treatments of Mexican culture and virtually nothing on the culture of the urban middle and upper class from which come the overwhelming majority of Mexican students in the United States. We know a great deal about the Indian village, but very little about the other 80 per cent of Mexico and virtually nothing about the city. Consequently, it is necessary to make a preliminary and necessarily provisional formulation of the major features of urban middle and upper class culture. This formulation is drawn from a variety of sources.[1] Not a little of our information came from our student subjects. A significant contribution was made by members of a graduate seminar which devoted a year to culling pertinent information from the literature on Mexico. Much represents formal organization of many years of observation, experience, and study on the part of the authors and the more intimate understanding of a staff

[1] Gordon Hewes, "Mexicans in Search of 'The Mexican,'" *American Journal of Economics and Sociology*, 13:209–23 (January 1954), reviews some Mexican literature attempting to define Mexican character. Some of his materials are drawn upon here.

member of Mexican ancestry. In the following discussion only the major conclusions will be presented.

All observers and students tend to emphasize the heterogeneity of Mexican culture, both in terms of class and of region. In colonial times the great estates of the south, peopled with Indian tributaries; the sugar plantations of the lowland areas, early worked by Negro slaves; the great mission establishments with functioning Indian communities; the mines of the center and north; the great cattle ranches of the north — these created different types of societies and different kinds of men.[2]

Regional, class, and rural-urban differences still characterize Mexico. In addition Mexico has undergone a major social revolution in the past forty years and any attempt to define themes, values, or attitudes must reckon with a time dimension that may introduce enormous contradictions. As in thirty years much of Mexico has moved from pack train to motor truck and airplane, so Mexican society has moved from a feudal society toward an industrial society.[3] The traditional elite has been destroyed, impoverished, or relegated to positions of little power or influence.

Mexican culture, then, derives from Spanish and Indian cultures, from the influence of later European and North American cultures, and from its own internal development and environmental conditions. It is unnecessary for us here to attempt to disentangle these various historical threads that enter into the fabric of contemporary Mexico. To understand the Mexican student we need only to understand the contemporary symbolism which may enable us to identify different ideological positions. Here it is perhaps enough to observe that contemporary Mexican ideology derives from the following complex sources: (1) a humanistic outlook in contrast to Puritanism; (2) an intellectual emphasis on logic and dialectics rather than on pragmatism; (3) an intellectual content deriving from such contradictory sources as the philosophers of the Age of Enlightenment, the French and American revolutions, capitalism, Catholic thought and philosophy, Marxism, and Spanish individualism.

[2] See, for example, François Chevalier, *La formation des grands domaines au Méxique. Terre et Société aux XVIe–XVIIe siècles* (Paris: Travaux et memoires de L'Institute d'Ethnologie, LVI, 1952).

[3] Some may not accept the use of the word "feudal" in this connection. We have used the term not to refer to a specific type of European society but to denote predominantly agrarian societies with very little social or occupational mobility, with power and wealth concentrated in a small traditional elite, and with a relatively fixed system of reciprocal obligations and rights.

To be understood, these historical influences must be viewed in the light of the Mexican revolution of 1910 which produced social changes of great magnitude. Full comprehension of contemporary Mexico requires a knowledge of the background of the revolution, its political-economic orientations, and the measures taken to reject, obstruct, or realize its basic objectives. The problems arising from the revolution are apparently the causes of major personal conflicts in the lives of some of the Mexican students we studied. Consideration of these is not without significance for students from some other countries, for with or without the violence that characterized the Mexican social revolution, similar social changes are in train in much of Latin America and indeed in all pre-industrial and essentially feudal societies.

Although the rate and direction of change are not the same for all sections of Mexican society, up to the end of the Cárdenas regime in 1940 the Mexican revolution was predominantly a nationalistic, agrarian reform movement, which viewed industrialization with suspicion and as something to be permitted only under the most rigid controls. The agrarian reforms did much to remove the economic base of the old landholding elite, and destroyed the previous political oligarchy.

The election of President Avila Camacho, successor to President Lázaro Cárdenas, coincided with a new phase in the revolution. "Since 1940 the center of attention has shifted sharply from agriculture to industry. In a few years' time Mexico has made great headway in establishing a base for a full-scale industrial development, already an impressive achievement though the process is just at the beginning stages." [4] This new movement has in a sense widened the gulf between the rural masses and the increasingly industrial urban population. A considerable number of Mexico's people still live virtually outside the national economy, supporting themselves by subsistence agriculture and handicraft production of most of the necessities of life. Nevertheless, among almost all groups improved communications and educational facilities have created desires for new goods and services associated with the modern industrial world. Growing population, deterioration of the land, and failure to improve the productive capacities of large sectors of the rural population have created widespread frustrations. "Agrarian reform has, however, produced social and political changes without concomitant changes in the technological order;

[4] Sanford Mosk, *The Industrial Revolution in Mexico* (Berkeley: University of California Press, 1950), p. vii.

11

the redistribution of land can neither change the technology nor supply needed credit." [5]

As the early agrarian phase of the revolution created a new political oligarchy and destroyed much of the economic base of the traditional elite, the rising industrialization has created a new type of urban capitalist who exercises important social and political controls. The rapid enlargement of the middle class and the emergence of new bases for prestige and leadership — new, that is, to Mexican society — are progressing so rapidly that a clear picture of the urban middle and upper classes is difficult.

Many broad institutional areas of Mexican culture present significant differences from the United States. Some of these may be characterized as follows:

1. *Politics and Government.* Political leadership and governmental participation are marked by a group of professional politicians and the influence of a growing bureaucracy. Intellectuals participate to a greater extent and wield much more influence than in the United States. Despite the dominance of the one-party system, effective political democracy is growing. The expanding middle class is increasingly represented. Low salaries are reflected in the *mordida* (system of bribery). Most students deplored the *mordida* as a sign of the low political morality of Mexico. But Arturo Ortiz,[6] although he disliked the *mordida*, pointed out that it is perhaps a result of low salaries. He drew a comparison with tipping in a restaurant, where one tips 10 or 15 per cent or, if services are very good, 20 per cent of the bill.

2. *Economic Institutions.* There is extensive participation, both organized and informal, by business, industry, agriculture, and labor in the formation of government economic policy. Government regulation of and participation in economic life are extensive and may tend to prevent the accumulation of private capital to care for large-scale developmental needs. The failure or inability of private capital to provide credit facilities in many areas has led to the creation of government loan agencies. Until recently the dominant economic philosophy of government has been agrarian tinged with socialistic concepts, in part a reaction against domination by foreign capital. Economic problems and the implementation

[5] Eric R. Wolf, "Aspects of Group Relations in a Complex Society: Mexico," *American Anthropologist,* 58:1065–78 (December 1956).

[6] All names referring to students are pseudonyms. The names of smaller communities are also fictitious.

of economic philosophy enter importantly into political affairs. Increasingly prominent, however, is a new industrial and business philosophy.

3. Army. As in many Latin American countries, the military is an important political force, but in Mexico its role and power have been reduced. Increasingly the viewpoint of the army is dominated by progressive middle-class aspirations.

4. Religion. Most Mexicans are professed Catholics, but in rural areas much of the religious participation is of a folk character. Particularly in urban centers many Mexicans are indifferent toward religion, or, although still considering themselves devout Catholics, are strongly anti-clerical. Secularism pervades most aspects of urban society, particularly among the middle and upper classes and the military.

Separation of church and state is far more complete than in most Latin American countries, and efforts to limit the economic privileges and political power of the Catholic Church have occurred several times in Mexican history. Its economic privileges were drastically limited in the middle of the last century under President Benito Juárez. The 1910 revolution was strongly anti-clerical and some groups involved were anti-Catholic. Church organizations are now legally denied corporate status and hence may not own property; monastic foundations and religious schools are prohibited; public religious processions and the wearing of clerical garb on the streets are illegal; and the clergy must be citizens. Enforcement of these laws, never complete, in recent years has become more lax. It should be noted that the legal restrictions and regulations apply to all denominations and not only to the Catholic Church.

5. Education. Mass education has developed since the revolution. Its character is strongly influenced by the pragmatic philosophy of John Dewey, but higher education still retains much of the traditional Latin American pattern, with heavy emphasis on the humanities. However, sciences and the professions have undergone considerable development in the past twenty years, and university education moves increasingly toward North American patterns. At advanced levels both faculty and students tend to have a high interest and an active participation in politics.

6. Intellectual and Aesthetic Life. Intellectual and artistic pursuits have educational and political functions as well as aesthetic purposes. Literature and painting especially have tended to document and propagandize the changing purposes of the revolutionary movement and to support Mexican nationalism.

7. *The Family*. The family remains the basic social and economic unit of Mexico. It is the major agency for socialization of the child, particularly in inculcating that peculiarly Latin concept of *educación* (see page 21). Important class differences probably exist within the general Mexican type of family, but even in the urban setting the family tends to be of the extended type. Sons often remain economically dependent or involved in family enterprises. Not infrequently sons continue to live at home until middle age or until their children are too numerous to be accommodated in the ancestral home. Children's relations with aunts and uncles are intimate and their closest associates are often their cousins. Social functions within the home tend to include only relatives. Nepotism in government and business is common and expected. These patterns probably are strongest at the middle- and upper-class levels, but in urban settings there is some diminution of the patriarchal character of the family, coupled with rising social position for women. Disruption of traditional family patterns is sufficiently common today to be viewed with alarm by many conservative writers.

8. *Compadrazgo*. Possibly nowhere in the Latin-Catholic world has the godparent relationship been so elaborated as in Mexico. Not only does the child treat his godparents like true parents, but parents and godparents *(compadres)* treat each other like, and are often closer than, true siblings. The *compadrazgo* is an elaborate system that extends kinship behavior to a large number of unrelated individuals. The *compadrazgo* influence reaches into the highest levels of business and government. For example, the decision to extend the federal rural school system into an area may be determined by the fact that a local political leader is a *compadre* of the minister of education. In the urban setting there appears to be considerable tendency for the *compadrazgo* and the kinship group to coalesce: relatives increasingly are chosen as godparents.

The revolution, as indicated, has destroyed the political position, much of the economic power, and to some degree the social prestige of the traditional elite. The self-made man can rise high in Mexico today and a marked degree of mobility has replaced the relatively static pre-revolutionary society. A growing and increasingly influential business and professional middle class merges imperceptibly into the group that today controls the wealth and political power of Mexico. The class picture, however, is still obscure, and concepts of prestige, status, and role functions would probably be more useful for a thorough analysis of Mexican society than concepts of class.

Despite the egalitarian philosophy of the revolution, reference to class and status differences and the ascription of behavior on this basis run constantly through the speech of every Mexican. Many of the referents and the symbols of status apparently operate at the subconscious level. Individuals will deny the existence or the validity of certain status distinctions and status symbols, yet use them in almost the next sentence. Mexico is still a strongly class- or status-conscious culture; but by comparison with other Latin American countries one sees the great magnitude of the change that has occurred in Mexico in this respect and appreciates the increasing fluidity of the society.

Along with the social and economic changes of the revolution have come changes in value orientations. Among the old elite and in rural areas traditional values tend to persist. Wealth itself is not a symbol of success, but is sought for personal security and, often, in rural areas, to carry out the ritual obligations of the folk religion. In the Indian village of Cherán, "In terms of individual wealth, the basic concepts are those of rural Mexico. Wealth is primarily in land and silver." [7] In the mestizo village of Tzintzuntzan, "Though silver is known to be non-productive, for centuries it has been the symbol of wealth and to it there is an emotional attachment matched only by that to land." [8]

These values, insofar as they persist in the urban areas, possibly find their expression through investment in urban real estate, contributing to the overdevelopment of office and apartment property. But increasingly in urban Mexico, status differences are measured in terms of the pecuniary calculus. Everywhere one finds a grasping for money, the "fast buck" philosophy, the quick speculative big-return venture rather than the sound and long-run modest-profit enterprise, and a low level of business morality. The symbols of monetary success are the swarms of Cadillacs, the fabulous houses of such sections as Chapultepec Heights and San Angel, the private *fronton* courts (for ball games) corresponding to the Hollywood swimming pools, elaborate dress, and lavish public entertainment of friends in restaurants and clubs.

[7] Ralph L. Beals, *Cherán: A Sierra Tarascan Village* (Washington, D.C.: Smithsonian Institution, Institute of Social Anthropology, Publication No. 2, 1956).

[8] George M. Foster, *Empire's Children: The People of Tzintzuntzan* (Washington, D.C.: Smithsonian Institution, Institute of Social Anthropology, Publication No. 6, 1948), p. 169.

Although the Mexican students come mainly from the upper middle class, few appear to belong to families of "excessive strivers." If they are aware of the contradiction posed by the existence of such strivers in Mexican society with their rejection of American materialism, they rationalize the "excessive strivers" as a small atypical group, or argue that the goals of the strivers still are ultimately secure family position and freedom to make possible a more "spiritual" concern with life and its meaning.

TRADITIONAL VALUES

In this section we will attempt to describe some of the leading themes and value orientations found among the urban upper class and in some parts of the middle class. No systematic effort is made to identify themes or value orientations of other class groups or to distinguish rural or regional differences. Some of the themes discussed are diminishing in importance or are undergoing modification. Several themes seem to be entirely rejected by some of the younger generation. A few themes are described which are not influential among upper and middle classes but which are well known to them. It should be noted that many of the themes or dominant orientations described by Mexican writers as reviewed by Hewes [9] are not included, for the Mexican writers apparently see the dominant pattern of Mexico in terms of the more numerous lower class.

The use here of the term "themes" conforms to the definition proposed by Morris Opler: "The term themes is used here in a technical sense to denote a postulate or position, declared or implied, and usually controlling behavior or stimulating activity, which is tacitly approved or openly promoted in a society." [10] Some of these themes have been identified by us but the majority have been mentioned in one form or another by Mexican writers or by our student subjects. In some cases widely known Mexican terms exist.

In a later section will be listed some newer or possibly emergent themes, many of which are contradictory to those here presented. As Opler pointed out in the article cited, contradictions are often apparent even among the traditional themes. On the other hand, many of the themes complement one another and are interrelated. This is particularly evident in the first group, which deals with familial-sexual relationships.

[9] Hewes, *op. cit.*
[10] Morris Edward Opler, "Themes as Dynamic Forces in Culture," *American Journal of Sociology,* 51:198–206 (November 1945).

First loyalty is owed to the family. The family means both the immediate family and the extended family, often including the *compadres*. Familial solidarity is one of the strongest traditional values in Mexican culture, particularly at middle- and upper-class levels, even among urban people. It is proper that a man in a position of power in government or business use his influence to secure jobs for his nephews, nieces, brothers, and cousins. Women wear mourning for the death of any relative, often for as long as a year for a distant cousin. In the most traditional families, women virtually spend their lives in mourning. The family was traditionally of primary importance for the ascription of status and it still has great significance.

The strength of the family, especially as extended by the *compadrazgo,* may well be a determinant of the neutral and even hostile attitudes toward friendship expressed by most Mexican students. A proper friendship is very deep and intimate and carries with it much the same loyalties one owes to the family. But such a close friend is very apt to become a *compadre* and hence be drawn into the formal family structure.

José Iturriaga considers Mexicans to have much less developed "social personalities" than North Americans; hence they are constrained in social relationships outside the family. He suggests that the *compadrazgo* is in part a compensation for this characteristic and that loyalties to persons tend to outweigh loyalty to ideas.[11] In the urban setting relatives tend increasingly to be selected as godparents of children. In such cases the *compadrazgo,* rather than extending family-like bonds, serves rather to reinforce the family by increasing its functions and maintaining solidarity against disruptive urban forces.

Men are superior to women and require a freer sex life. The father is the authoritarian head of the household. He has exceptional powers of discipline. While the wife is cloistered, the husband may have mistresses or a series of promiscuous relationships without real danger of divorce. The expression *todo un hombre* (every bit a man) bears a deep meaning in Mexican culture. In part the double standard is related to the general attitudes toward women outlined below. In part it results from a belief in the necessity of sexual activity to the health of the male. Informants describe as typical the concern of the father or the older brother to initiate young males into sex life properly. Sometimes the older relative

[11] José E. Iturriaga, *La Estructura Social y Cultural de México* (Mexico City: Fondo de Cultura Economica, 1951), p. 234.

17

will take a boy in his teens to a prostitute. Alternatively, sometimes the father will arrange for an experienced older woman to be the boy's mistress until he has learned to manage his own sex life. Wives know and accept this. Thus, although Isabella López feels that in more educated classes the older patterns are breaking down, the normal pattern still is for the husband to "expect you to be at home with the children, and then have a *casa chica* [little house]. [The] *casa grande* [big house] is the house for your wife, and then you have a mistress in a small apartment, and that's the *casa chica,* and that is quite common in certain circles; women know about it and expect it. And I think any girls in my own circle and in my own generation would accept that sort of thing." She identifies this with the Catholic idea "that the husband is the one who has all the say and the woman just has to comply with anything he does, anything he says; it doesn't make any difference if it's wrong, the woman doesn't even have the right to judge him. But I think that most of the girls of my own generation would accept this philosophy."

The mother is the center of the home. The woman's role is defined as "kitchen, church, and children." The mother symbolizes purity. Her submissive role before the husband draws her to a closer relationship with the children for validation of her existence. She forms strong ties with her sons, to whom she looks for moral sustenance and economic support if widowed. Mexican motion pictures abound in tear-jerking sentimentality about the relations between mother and son. Over her sons the mother exerts no disciplinary authority. Without significant exceptions, male students denied any conflicts with their mothers.

Siblings must support one another. Mutual respect obtains among sibs. A brother holds a distinctive respect for the sister and is honor-bound to defend her from insult. Brothers carefully supervise a girl's contacts with males. Deferential respect is paid to the eldest brother, who may exercise parental disciplinary and protective functions even in the father's presence. Sons and father avenge each other's wrongs and form a bloc against external threat.

Love is both tragic and romantic. Women are viewed as inherently unfaithful, a derivative of Renaissance and Arabic views that love is a disease of the passions. Women are both weak and passionate and hence without aid they are unable to protect their virtue. "Good" women, therefore, must be sequestered and supervised. Women and money may be linked as evil forces conspiring the ruin of the male. Love is a profound human experience. The Mexican would not sing, "I found a million dollar baby in a five-and-ten-cent store." He conceives of love in an almost mystical sense. Sex, of course, is something else — a necessity to every male.

Race, caste, and class are important determinants of status and character. Race consciousness is primarily found in the traditional elite which denies and looks down upon any Indian mixture. It mainly finds its expression in the tracing of family lines and in insistence upon the purity of the blood. The concept has been of limited influence in Mexico since the scandals of colonial times when there was a lively traffic in forged certificates of *limpieza de la sangre* which guaranteed freedom not only from Indian but from Moorish and Jewish "blood." (Originally the certificates were a security clearance, guaranteeing an uncontaminated *religious* background; the euphemistic phrasing acquired wider meaning.) Class is more important than race, but there is a high correlation between low class status and having Indian "blood." The traditional elite hardened this to a caste line.

La raza is the source of spiritual unity. The concept of *la raza* is essentially mystical. *La raza* has little to do with race; rather it is an idealization and glorification of Latin culture as opposed to Anglo-Saxon culture. *Por mi espíritu hablará mi raza* (through my spirit my race will speak) may be as powerfully influential a phrase to a mestizo or even an Indian as it is to a person claiming unblemished descent from Christian Spain.

One should always defend la patria. The feeling for *la patria,* the fatherland, seems to have been connected with the independence movement and was strongest in immediately pre-revolutionary Mexico. In practice *la patria* tends to mean the state or region, except when an external threat arouses the higher loyalty to the nation. The extreme expression is found in the *patriotero,* the hundred-percenter, who insists all things Mexican. are superior.

Things foreign are always superior. Mexicans name this *malinchismo,* derived from Malinche, the native woman who became assistant and mistress to Cortez. In colonial times superiority was attributed to things Spanish. In the nineteenth century *malinchismo* was primarily admiration for things French. In modern times anyone who expresses undue admiration for anything foreign is apt to be accused of *malinchismo.* The extreme *malinchista* is the antithesis of the *patriotero.*

The old ways were better. In extreme form this is a restricted theme known today as *porfirismo* and tends to be associated with *malinchismo*. *Porfirismo* is a more modern term dating from the revolution, and refers to individuals who believe that all things were better in the days of Don Porfirio Díaz, last dictator before the revolution. As Díaz frequently is accused, perhaps with some justice, of having sold out Mexico to foreign interests and of having greater regard for foreigners than for Mexicans, the linkage with *malinchismo* is clear. Some Mexican students in the study may be labeled *porfiristas,* while all are subject to, and apprehensive of, being accused of *malinchismo* on their return home.

Religion is the basis of society and the moral order. All things happen as God wills. He sanctions the social order and dispenses punishment and rewards. All are sinners except small children and must undergo punishment for sin. But true repentance can bring forgiveness, and punishment in the afterlife may be lightened by the supplication of the living expressed in prayer. The concept of God the Father reinforces the traditional authoritarian family structure. The parallel is further reinforced by the great popularity of the cult of the Virgin, the always-forgiving and understanding mother.

To lead the good life one must have non-material goals. Life is meant to be lived. Time, work, and money, consequently, do not have value in themselves. Certain kinds of work are degrading (for example, most work with the hands), and those who perform such tasks lack spiritual and intellectual sensitivity. Spiritual and intellectual matters are more important than material. Honor hence may be given the scholar, even though he is poor and without family, if he has *educación* (proper behavior, see page 21). The wealthy and status-conscious intellectual who cannot carry a package on the street may perform prodigies of literary production. Mexican (and European) cultures are spiritual; Anglo-Saxons (especially North Americans) are materialistic. The word is, therefore, superior to the deed.

There is little concern about parceling activity by the clock and time is not a commodity. The maxims of Benjamin Franklin are alien to Mexican culture. "Remember that time is money. He that can earn ten shillings a day by his labor, and goes abroad . . . He that idly loses five shillings worth of time, loses five shillings and might as prudently throw five shillings into the sea." Rather the Mexican says, *Hay mas tiempo que vida* (There is more time than life). The urban middle-class Mexican, however, increasingly recognizes the value of punctuality in business and professional activities, although not in private life. This theme, moreover, has its greatest potency among those with means, but it is not without significance for lower-class persons who refuse to work to pay for future needs.

Educación is the basis of social approval. A person is often said to be *instruida* but without *educación.* This means that while he may have a formal education, yet he does not honor his family and conduct himself properly in social relations. Reciprocal respect is the basis of *educación* patterns but must be accompanied by behavior appropriate to class and status: an uneducated peasant may have *educación.* Wealth or distinguished achievement gain social recognition only when accompanied by *educación.*

Ritual is to be valued. Related to the emphasis on *educación,* the Mexican values formality in behavior in accordance with circumstances. Obvious in church rites, in the fiesta, in public events such as the bull fight, ritual also marks interpersonal relations as in the introduction patterns, ceremonial hand-shaking, insistence on precedence, the elaborate use of titles, and avoidance of informal terms of address. Mexicans are regarded as stuffily formal by many other Latin Americans, although not by all.

Death is to be accepted, or death is present in life. Anglo-Saxons seal themselves from death as they engage fiercely in worldly activity. Mexicans, it may be said, make a frontal approach to death, consciously and with courage; the women supported by prayer and ritual and the men armed with a concept of personal honor. Mexicans neither admit fear of death nor sentimentalize it.

In this connection Hewes[12] suggests that one product of the inferiority feelings attributed to the Mexican by many Mexican writers is the building up of fantasies in which one is a hero or a saint. He points out that as Xavier Tavera has noted, "to do this one must die, and death is the ultimate means to salvage personal prestige." In both prehistoric and modern Mexico the death motif is common. Hewes refers to Tavera's mention of the "morbid eagerness" of Mexican medical students in dissection and discusses the precise details published in newspapers of traffic fatalities, the elaboration of funeral rites, and the elaborate celebration of the Day of the Dead. Hewes believes the popularity of bull fighting is associated with this attitude.

This analysis seems incomplete, for the observances on the Day of the

[12] Hewes, *op. cit.,* pp. 218–19.

Dead often are not morbid. Rather there is an acceptance of death, a strong and pleasant feeling of communion with those who have died, and an absence of sentimentality in the celebration which is a far cry from attitudes in the United States.

Life is to be lived dramatically. Mexicans love action, movement, color, and sound. The haggling of the market place, the extravagant audience behavior at the bull fight, the love of adventure and daring, the wealth of flowers from palace to hovel, are all expressions of this set of values. Nothing damns a village so much as to have said of it *No hay movimiento* (Nobody is stirring) and nearly every foreign commentator emphasizes the noisiness of Mexico. Indeed, the abuses of the sound truck, the loud-speaker, and the radio suggest that Mexico's traditional love of music is partly love of noise.

Music is a true expression of Mexico. Mestizo folk music is the most representative and most consistent expression of Mexican music. Both folk songs and the lyrics of modern popular songs refer constantly to dominant themes in Mexican culture. Mexicans are deeply, emotionally responsive to Mexican music; even sophisticates who profess to scorn the shoddiness of much contemporary popular music succumb to the authentic folk music. A recent attempt to bar strolling musicians from overcrowded buses in Mexico City aroused a storm of public indignation.

The universe is hierarchically ordered. Most interpersonal and economic relationships have an authoritarian structure. Problems and decisions are constantly referred to authority. Such relationships as the father-family, priest-parishioner, *patrón-peón*, professor-student, political leader–follower all have this characteristic. The grown son accepts the father's decision, the worker seeks a "good" *patrón* as the answer to his problems, the student does not question the professor, the political leader builds a personal following rather than an ideological movement. The indignant newspaper editorial or magazine article ends, not with a call to action on the part of readers, but with a referral of the problem to authority: "The government should . . ." Opportunity and success in business and government are widely assumed to depend upon knowing or being related to the right people. Hewes suggests that the conceptual framework of Adorno and Frenkel-Brunswik's "authoritarian personality" fits many if not all described Mexican character traits.[13]

The individual personality is to be valued. This is an extreme form

[13] *Ibid.*, p. 222.

22

of non-economically motivated individualism, derived from but not identical with Spanish *egoismo*. It is related to the Catholic view that not only is each man endowed with a soul but all souls are equal in the eyes of God. Each man's soul, however, is his own concern and the universe, the events in it, and the actions and speech of others are constantly evaluated in relation to one's personality. The strong sense of honor is operative here and face must be saved at all costs. Sensitivity to criticism is high and criticism in public or even before a third person evokes strong response. Iturriaga speaks of "excessive self-pride" which he associates with the high rate of crimes of violence (second highest homicide rate, crimes of violence four times greater than crimes against property), a sharp sensitivity to ridicule, and unsociable individualistic attitudes.[14]

A real man is muy macho. Machismo seems never to have been completely accepted by all Mexicans and possibly is a disappearing pattern. It is a purely masculine set of values and might, somewhat misleadingly, be translated as "manliness." It calls for aggressive sexuality, reckless bravery, and hair-trigger sensitivity toward "honor." Its blatant form does not appear in the urban upper or middle classes, but all the subsidiary values operate in some degree. Thus police in Mexico City allowed one of the drunken prisoners arrested in a disturbance in a fashionable night club to keep his pistol when he claimed that to surrender it would reflect upon his honor. Hewes notes that the image of the Mexican in the rest of Latin America is that of the "swaggering, hyper-masculine hero, the glamorous *charro* — an image summed up in the word *Jorge Negretismo*.[15] (The *charro* is the idealized cowboy, a part played frequently by the late Jorge Negrete, Mexico's most popular motion picture idol.) But the recurring "strong man," the *caudillo,* in Latin American politics often shows the qualities of *machismo*.

Manual labor is degrading. Low social status is associated with manual labor. There is no concept of work as an end in itself, or as a discipline. Work is not generally rewarding. To have servants is a necessary validation of high social status. Intellectual, scientific, and directive activities alone carry prestige. To do housework, to carry burdens of any sort, even to work in one's garden threatens status.

Success is measured in traditional terms. Traditionally achievement and success rest on the validation of ascribed status on the basis of having

[14] Iturriaga, *op. cit.,* p. 233.
[15] Hewes, *op. cit.,* p. 213.

economic security without effort, being considered *gente decente* by virtue of conformance to the dominant themes, and acquiring prestige and status symbols such as land ownership, positions in social and religious organizations, intellectual achievement, power and influence, money and family — with varying emphases and combinations. Traditionally an individual with *educación* might rise to higher status but only in recent times could this raise the status of his family.

EMERGENT VALUES

The emergent values of Mexico are less clearly defined. Often movement away from traditional values is apparent but the substitutes are not yet elaborated or clearly defined. Substitute values are often held only by limited groups, and it is too soon to predict their general acceptance with certainty. There is, however, a decided movement toward the urban-industrial values widely held in western European and North American cultures; these seem to comprise a considerable segment of the emergent values. The following items are merely suggestive.

Mexico must become an integrated nation. The 1910 revolution, the active desire to create a sovereign nation — principally by destroying the quasi-colonial economic status through national ownership of natural resources and by industrialization, and the historical nature of United States–Mexican relations, all have given a very sharp edge to Mexican nationalism. The character and significance of this nationalism will emerge more clearly in the discussion of preconceptions of Mexican students about the United States.

An important new theme related to nationalism is *indigenismo,* a product of the revolution. It consists of identification with, and to some extent glorification of, the Indian, particularly the Indian past. It is no accident that Mexico spends a larger proportion of its national revenue on archaeological research than perhaps any other country in the world. In the abstract, very few Mexican students express antagonism toward the Indian or the Indian cultures; many, on the other hand, either regret that they are not Indian or express pride in having Indian ancestry. Iturriaga emphasized the contrast between Peru and Mexico.[16] In the first country the national hero is Pizarro, while in Mexico the national symbol is Cuautemoc, last leader of the Aztec resistance. Hewes points out the indoctrination of the Mexican child from his early years; elementary textbooks,

---

[16] Iturriaga, *op. cit.,* pp. 226–27.

in describing the war of the conquest, contain such sentences as "Here we defeated the Spaniards." [17]

Related to, but to some extent in opposition to extreme forms of *indigenismo,* is the movement to "incorporate the Indian into national life," one of the revolutionary slogans. So long as the Indian masses do not participate effectively in the national life, they are seen as an obstacle to the development of a national culture and a modern state. Despite verbal commitments on an abstract level, in concrete situations most students do in fact look down upon the Indian.

Mexico must participate independently in international affairs. Such international market arrangements as the cartels that threatened Mexican oil, World War II and Mexico's military and economic participation, the Korean war, the rise of Soviet power, and United States-Russian hostility, all combine with the particular direction of Mexican development to give marked international awareness to Mexican government and politics.

For many Mexicans, self-esteem is closely involved with national status. Hence Mexicans chafe under the knowledge that a foreign policy completely independent of the United States is impossible. At the same time they aspire toward leadership of the Spanish-American countries. As Mexico now is or will soon become the largest Spanish-speaking country in the world in population as it already is in area, strivings for independence and international leadership will be intensified.

Education is the hope of Mexico. Mass education as an instrument of progress has become a positive value for at least a sizable minority of all classes. This is a marked departure from earlier advocacy of a classical education for the elite only. For segments of the lower class, education still lacks value. This is particularly true in rural villages where parents still believe children will follow the life patterns of previous generations. Rejection of education is associated with the belief in a static society.

Industrialization and social change are desirable. Determination to "build a steel and concrete civilization" is accompanied by the belief that this will solve Mexico's problems and by a rejection of the belief in a static society. This emergent theme is especially prevalent among spokesmen for urban labor, as well as for business and industry.

Art is part of life. Contemporary art is in part a product of the revolutionary period. Artists tend to be political minded, mural art is for the

[17] Hewes, *op. cit.,* p. 211.

masses, and Mexican thought and feeling are communicated through artistic work on public buildings.

THE PROBLEM OF TYPOLOGY

Mexican culture is in transition, but the direction of its movement is not yet uniform and establishment of a typology of theme or value patterns is difficult. No division on the basis of adherence to traditional versus modern values is adequate. The adherence of individual Mexicans to various cultural themes differs in a number of categories but individual patterns show little consistency. We cannot, for example, state that a person who is clearly a *porfirista,* that is, one who wishes to return to the social and economic conditions of pre-revolutionary Mexico, will necessarily be a devout or "fanatic" (to use a Mexican term) Catholic. Not infrequently, indeed, he may be rather strongly anti-clerical. In other words, placing a Mexican along one dimension of values and attitudes has relatively low predictive value for his position upon another dimension.

We do not intend fully to elaborate this problem in this monograph, but some further illustration may be desirable. For example, certain polar clusters of social, political, and economic values can be identified. One, which we have called the urban-industrialist, includes those who are firmly committed to building a "steel and concrete civilization." Another includes the "old revolutionists" or the agrarian revolutionists, dedicated to agrarian reform as the basic need of Mexico. The third are the traditionalists or *porfiristas.*

These three clusters do not represent a linear series but rather a tri-polar distribution with many individuals falling somewhere between the poles. The situation is further complicated by the fact that each of these poles has a liberal or radical-conservative continuum related to it. Thus an urban-industrialist may be either a Marxist labor leader or the equivalent of a conservative United States industrialist. A traditionalist may either believe in a return to pre-revolutionary days in all respects, or believe a gradual development from a pre-revolutionary base would have been the soundest progress.

In religious attitudes and behaviors we can readily identify six different types or modes of expression: the "fanatic" favoring the domination of the Catholic Church over the state; the devout believer and church attendant accepting some separation of church and state; the liberal who favors a greater social action role for the Catholic Church; the anti-clerical who accepts the faith but rejects the institutional domination of the Catholic Church; Protestants; and nonreligious. Because of the small numbers involved, we have included together in the last category not only nonreligious but anti-religious and non-Christians. The latter are mostly of Jewish or Buddhist faith. All these groups are identifiable in Mexican history since the establishment of the Republic and some were present in colonial times.

Students may also be classified according to their goals. Some students have primarily practical goals, here defined as entry into business or industry, the professions, government bureaucracy, or social action programs. Others have primarily intellectual goals defined here as teaching, writing, and research.

Most of the students for whom we have data could be described in terms of these variables but for purposes of illustration we will confine the discussion to the ten students interviewed at UCLA who can be described with most confidence. The relation of these students to the variables selected as of the time of our study is shown in Table 1.

Table 1. Placement of 10 Students Interviewed at UCLA with Respect to Selected Variables

Student	Socio-Political and Economic Orientation	Religious Mode	Radical-Conservative Orientation	Goals
A	Urban-industrial	Liberal Catholic	Conservative	Practical
B	Urban-industrial	Liberal Catholic	Conservative	Practical
C	Agrarian revolutionary	Liberal Catholic	Moderate radical	Intellectual
D	Agrarian revolutionary	Liberal Catholic	Conservative	Intellectual
E	Agrarian revolutionary	Nonreligious	Liberal	Intellectual
F	Agrarian revolutionary	Nonreligious	Moderate radical	Intellectual
G	Agrarian revolutionary	Nonreligious	Moderate radical	Intellectual
H	Agrarian revolutionary	Nonreligious	Radical	Practical
I	Traditional	Devout Catholic	Liberal	Intellectual
J	Traditional	Nonreligious	Conservative	Intellectual

Although Table 1 covers only a limited number of students, it conveys a partial idea of the complexities to be encountered in developing a typology. One deficiency of the table is that it does not show changes revealed in the life histories of these students. Student E, for example, before coming to the United States, had shifted from a traditional to an agrarian revolutionary orientation and from devout Catholic, to fanatic, to non-religious. Student J had shifted from anti-clerical to anti-religious.

If all student subjects had been included, several additional combinations would be apparent. A number of Protestants and anti-clericals would be found to be associated with several different combinations of variables. One or two students may have been fanatic Catholics, although we hesitate to make this identification solely from our written materials for the basic attitudes and ideologies associated with this religious mode make it very unlikely that many fanatic Catholics will study in the United States. We further believe that one theoretically possible combination, the traditionalist who is also a Protestant, is extremely rare in Mexico if it exists at all.

This sample analysis serves to place the important group of students intensively interviewed within the context of several significant aspects of Mexican culture. The analysis also indicates that a typology involving a large number of students and including most of the important variables would be exceedingly complex. This is a reflection of the heterogeneity and rapid rate of change in Mexico. It also is a reflection of the fact that the directions of change are not yet clear-cut and that individuals are changing at uneven rates with respect to different aspects of the culture.

THE MEXICAN EDUCATIONAL SYSTEM

As with so much else in Mexico, the educational system is in a state of change. Before the revolution of 1910 the educational system was designed primarily for a small elite and the curriculum was classical and traditional in character. Most of the few elementary schools were in the cities and the bulk of the population was illiterate. The curriculum was arranged to pass the student through a series of steps by examinations, culminating in a university degree. Scientific and technical education was at a minimum. The National University dominated higher education and trained people in the humanities or in law, medicine, or civil engineering. A few schools, mainly charitable or religious, taught trades such as shoe-making or carpentry to a limited number of children of the lower class.

During this period few persons not of the aristocratic upper class had opportunities for advanced study. Exceptions were usually individuals adopted or sponsored by upper-class families. Foreign study was not uncommon for upper-class youth, and France and Spain were the preferred countries, establishing a tradition still strong in Mexico. Nevertheless, during this time some Mexican youths studied in England and in the United States. It is not without significance, perhaps, that Francisco I. Madero, member of a wealthy aristocratic landowning family in northern Mexico and initiator of the Mexican revolution, studied at the University of California.

Since the revolution a great expansion and modernization of the elementary school system has taken place. Tens of thousands of rural schools have been built and urban facilities have multiplied greatly. A shortage of properly trained teachers has limited the effectiveness of this program and rural schools frequently offer only two to four years. Rural students who complete six years of elementary school and who wish to continue are either sent to schools in the city or, more commonly, attend vocational schools in rural areas, in which agriculture is the most important subject. In general the facilities as well as the curriculums offered in the rural schools do not prepare students for university-level work. Few Mexican students in our sample had attended rural schools, even at the elementary level. In urban centers, although some elementary schools are vocationally oriented, many prepare students for secondary schools.

In both rural and urban elementary schools, despite the strong influence of John Dewey on Mexican education since the revolution, instruction tends to be authoritarian and to place heavy emphasis upon memory. During study periods students learn long passages, repeating them aloud. Consequently, at a distance even a one-room rural school at times will sound like a hive of angry bees. Recitation often consists of the class's repeating in unison passages learned word by word; and final public examinations, which often are oral, may consist of rote responses to fixed questions by the students with the best memories, interspersed with musical selections by the village band and speeches by local dignitaries.

After leaving the six-year elementary school, the student may enter a three-year *secundária,* sometimes called a *colégio.* Curriculums there too are somewhat classical and traditional, discipline is strict, attendance is watched, and examinations are frequent. Some secondary schools are more technical and graduation from them may lead directly to work in

29

some curriculums of the National Polytechnic Institute or such institutions as the National School of Agriculture. In the better *secundárias* instruction in mathematics, science, and sometimes other subjects often is more advanced than at similar grade levels in the United States.

Before admission to university curriculums, the student spends three additional years (formerly two years) in an accredited preparatory school or in preparatory schools maintained by the National University or the Polytechnic Institute. Before entering the university the student normally has received a *bachillerato,* equivalent to the high school diploma, for twelve years of schooling. Mexicans often identify the *bachillerato* with the bachelor's degree and hence equate the United States undergraduate college with the preparatory school.

A considerable number of students attend private elementary schools and *colégios,* run either by various language-nationality groups in Mexico or by religious orders. The American High School in Mexico City is an example. Many of these schools are not accredited for entrance to Mexican universities; graduates of these schools hence are pushed toward study in the United States and a substantial number of these are included in our sample.

At the university level, education both past and present has been dominated by the national university. Although state or regional universities have existed, some of them for a very long time, in the past their standards were low. Recently the quality and number of these institutions have increased.

University instruction tends to be somewhat formal and specialized. The student, by the time he reaches the university, is regarded as responsible and attendance at lectures is not enforced. Examinations usually occur only at the end of a semester or year. Curriculums tend to be rigid and offer few optional courses. Most university professors hold other jobs and they normally spend little time at the university outside the scheduled class hours. Classes often meet irregularly. Lectures tend to be formal and authoritarian. Discussion is rare and laboratory, demonstration, or case methods have been used only recently and not in all fields.

The grading patterns are quite different and vary from subject to subject. Some professional degrees, such as one in engineering, are given. In other fields the student who has completed a course of study may receive the *licenciate.* In some fields this means literally that he is licensed to follow a given profession. In some cases an intermediate status of *pasante* may be granted, meaning that the student has completed all required course work satisfactorily but must write a thesis before receiving the *licenciate*.

Some curriculums may exceed four years in length; medicine, for example, requires five years. In others, advanced degrees may be obtained by graduate study, although the doctorate is still not frequent outside the field of medicine. Some schools are attempting to approximate the M.A. and Ph.D. requirements of American universities, but on the whole this is a relatively recent development.

The value of a period of foreign study or a foreign degree varies markedly depending upon the field of study. There is a long tradition of foreign study in Mexico, particularly study at European universities. Until recently most students abroad studied humanities, with the goal of acquiring a liberal education. French medical degrees also were preferred and the French approach to medicine still dominates part of the profession.

With increasing industrialization, especially since World War II, interest in technical training has increased. The student with ambitions in most technical fields usually prefers to study in the United States, but Europe still has a strong appeal, especially for students with humanistic interests. It is a fair observation, though, that many present or potential leaders in scholarly, professional, and technical fields have received part of their training in the United States. Although many members of the upper-class groups are conscious of the need for foreign training, the public at large does not share this view and foreign study does not necessarily advance a student's career on return.

In not a few professional fields foreign degrees are not recognized and must be revalidated. This is particularly true where licensing qualifications are established by law. However, it is impossible to generalize about the effects of foreign training, for much depends upon the attitudes and personnel of the place where the student finds employment. Sometimes he finds he must play down his foreign training for he is regarded with some suspicion, and if he makes suggestions it may be felt he is trying to show his superiority. In other cases — and some of the notable ones are in research or government offices — preference may be given to individuals with recognizably better foreign training than can be obtained in Mexico. This is particularly apt to be true if the superior officers have also studied in the United States.

In summary, it may be observed that the Mexican undergraduate student comes to the United States university believing that he is prepared to specialize in his subject. He tends to resent the requirements that make him take courses outside his special field, and the compulsory attendance and frequent examinations which he associates with his secondary school background. Furthermore he is not prepared for the non-authoritarian presentation of many instructors. More advanced students who enter graduate schools are likely to be far more pleased with their initial experiences.

At both undergraduate and graduate levels, Mexican students vary widely in their preparation. Some may be good technicians but lack a general grasp of the field; others may have purely theoretical training. Few United States institutions seem to understand differences in the Mexican educational system, and excellently prepared students with a *licenciate* may be barred from graduate schools. Both in coming to the United States and in returning to Mexico the student usually encounters difficulties and frustrations in securing proper evaluation and recognition of his prior training.

The student's experience after his return depends upon his particular field of study. If he must validate his United States degree through examinations or attending courses, he is often better off if he gets a degree in Mexico first and then studies further in the United States without securing a degree. In other situations the United States degree may have high value.

2

The Mexican Student at Home

THE Mexican student arrives in the United States with extensive knowledge of his own culture and society. Over many years he has learned to recognize cues for behavior and has developed an extensive repertoire of more or less appropriate responses. He has developed attitude and value systems and learned to manipulate or adjust to a segment of the social structure of his own country. Much of his knowledge and experience has been thoroughly internalized and his behavioral responses to a host of life situations are relatively automatic.

On arrival in the United States the student not only must learn new cues and appropriate behavioral responses to them, but he discovers that many of his accepted cues call either for no response or for quite different responses. Deeply ingrained habits associated with the simplest aspects of daily living often must be modified or abandoned and new ones acquired. In anthropological terms he experiences a more or less severe cultural shock and, if he makes any tolerable adjustment, he must learn and internalize within a few months what his American fellow students have spent years in acquiring. What the student perceives in the United States — using perception in the broadest sense — and how he interprets and responds to what he perceives, are importantly influenced by his prior experience.

Personality factors unquestionably play an important part, both in decisions to study in the United States and in the adjustments the students make after arrival. Technically there seems no way of establishing prior personality factors with precision from retrospective data; hence such factors will be considered only superficially where they seem particularly relevant and reasonably clear. On the other hand, we can adequately establish the cultural and social background. Motivation to foreign study and prior knowledge and preconceptions of the United States will also be examined.

The analysis of Mexican culture in the first chapter was predicated upon the urban middle- and upper-class character of most Mexican students in our sample. Other similarly broad generalizations can be made. For example, all appeared to have had superior educational backgrounds. Many had previously traveled outside Mexico for noneducational purposes. The majority were male and Catholic. Such broad characterizations conceal important variations which must be examined and their meaning interpreted in Mexican terms.

ORIGINS OF MEXICAN STUDENTS

The overwhelming majority of our students came from the southern part of the Central Plateau or from the northern border tier of states.[1] With one exception, no member of the sample came from further south than a few miles south of Mexico City. Moreover, the most conservative central core of the Mexican plateau was unrepresented in our sample; no students came from such states as Zacatecas, Aguas Calientes, Hidalgo, or Guanajuato. Data on birthplace and place of prior education are summarized in Table 2. Of fifty-two respondents, one third, or seventeen, were born in Mexico City; twelve were born in urban communities away from the border, such places as Guadalajara, Puebla, and Mérida; five were born in urban communities in border states such as Monterrey, Chihuahua, and Guaymas; four were born in border towns which by many criteria are urban, such as Piedras Negras and Tijuana; three were born in the United States but returned to Mexico when quite small, while two were born in Europe but brought to Mexico by their parents while still of pre-school age.[2] Only nine, then, can be considered of small-town origin, from mainly agricultural communities. Most of these towns would be classed as urban according to the criteria used by the

---

[1] These and all subsequent statements are subject to the reservations concerning the sample as described in the Appendix. We believe the sample to be fairly representative, despite the many possible biasing factors. The geographical distribution of the members of the sample tends to bear this out, for it is congruent with such factors as the distribution of wealth, development of the educational system, contact with and acceptance of modern ideas, and the location of industrial development.

[2] Inclusion of these five students may be questioned; however, except for birthplace, the data from them seemed in all respects to fall within the range of the Mexican born.

United States census, but this is relatively meaningless in Mexico where most farmers live in towns. Four fifths or more of the students, then, were born in cities or large towns.

The educational histories of the subjects is perhaps more indicative of urban experience than birthplace (see Table 2). Of forty-eight students responding, twenty received all or part of their elementary education in Mexico City, only three in small towns. Two students who received part of their elementary education in the United States were from border towns and attended schools on the United States side of the border. Urban backgrounds become even more marked for secondary education. Of fifty-one students responding, twenty-five had all or part of their secondary education in Mexico City, only two in small towns, while fifteen received part of their secondary education in the United States. Many attended secondary schools in more than one location.

Table 2. Birthplace and Place of Prior Education

Place of Pre-United States Experience	Birthplace (N = 52)	Elementary Education (N = 48)	Secondary Education (N = 51)	University, Technical, Other Post-Secondary (N = 51)
Mexico City	17	20	25	18
Other cities (except those in border states)..	12	16	13	6
Cities in border states..	5	5	6	2
Border towns	4	5	4	0
Small towns	9	3	2	0
United States	3	2	15	16
Europe	2	0	0	0
Total	52	51*	65*	42†

* Total exceeds number of respondents because some respondents were educated in more than one place.

† Nine respondents reported no prior post-secondary education.

Forty-two students had attended technical or university-level schools in Mexico, or had attended some other advanced institution in the United States before becoming subjects of the study. Eighteen reported study in Mexico City, eight reported study in other urban centers, and sixteen (approximately one third) had attended other United States universities.

The essentially urban background of the Mexican student thus seems well established. Actually only three subjects were born in extremely rural or isolated locations. Of these, one had studied in Mexico City before coming to the United States, while another had spent a good deal of his life either in urban settings or in extensive travel with his parents. The third, who had apparently spent more of his life in a highly rural setting than any other of the fifty-two respondents, was born in the United States.

Establishment of the class origins of the students is difficult if the stratification criteria commonly used in the United States are mechanically employed. Judgments were formed by the staff of the project not only on the basis of father's income, occupation, and educational background, but family status, social participation, attitudes, and similar factors. But it must be remembered that the social structure of Mexico is in a highly fluid condition and the judgments are fallible. Possibly only one or two respondents were of the traditional upper class. Classification of the forty-four respondents for whom we felt we could make some judgment is shown in the tabulation.

Class	*No.*
Upper	1
Upper middle	25
Lower middle	14
Skilled worker	1
Peasant-laborer	3

Some upper-middle-class individuals might be regarded as upper class in United States' terms but by Mexican standards they lack sufficient family background. Those in the lower middle classification were so placed primarily because of the father's occupation and income. But the most significant observation is that the fathers of all forty middle- and upper-class individuals are in either white-collar occupations or a high government position, or professional or entrepreneurial and managerial activities. Of course, skilled workers have in the past been few in Mexico, and the low representation is to be expected. The peasant-laborer classification includes all whose fathers earn their living either by farming or doing manual labor requiring low skills. The importance of family position in establishing class membership makes the attempt to subdivide the upper levels extremely dubious.

The high economic standing of parents is reflected in the fact that twenty-one out of fifty students responding were wholly supported in their studies in the United States by their families. Thirteen were supported by fellowships. Sixteen were employed, and eleven of these were wholly self-supporting. Twenty out of thirty-nine respondents had been employed in Mexico before coming to the United States.

Relevant to the economic background of parents as well as to the general level of sophistication of students is the amount of foreign travel for noneducational purposes. Thirty-one out of forty-eight respondents had traveled outside Mexico. These figures conceal considerable variation, however. Prior travel in the United States by students from border states sometimes consisted of brief trips to recreational areas close to the border. (Simple visiting in border towns was not counted.) Some travel, on the other hand, was quite purposive. For example, one subject made his only prior trip to the United States by bus to visit medical schools before deciding where to study. Others had visited relatives in the United States, for twenty-one out of forty-seven respondents reported relatives living in this country.

In view of the restricted opportunities for advanced study in Mexico in the past, the education of relatives suggests that many students come from families which place a higher value on education than is usual in Mexico. Eighteen out of thirty-seven respondents reported their fathers had had some training after the secondary school level, and twenty-three out of thirty-nine reported siblings with post–secondary school education. Advanced education of mothers, uncles, wives, and fiancées was listed frequently.

More than half the respondents had attended one or more types of private school for all or part of both primary and secondary education. Of forty-seven responding, thirty had part of their primary school education in secular private schools, seven in religious schools, and nine in "foreign" schools. Thirty-one had part of their secondary school education in private schools, seven in religious schools, and ten in "foreign" schools. (By "foreign" schools is meant such institutions as the American High School in Mexico City, usually unaccredited by Mexican universities.) These data are summarized in Table 3.

While students in our sample were predominantly male, there was a higher proportion of women than is true among Mexican students generally since of the fifty-two respondents in the study twelve were female. This distortion results from the inclusion of students at Los Angeles City College, where there is an endowed residence hall for Mexican women students.

The assertion that the Mexican students were predominantly Catholic

Table 3. Type of School Attended (N = 47)

	Primary	Secondary
Public	22	28
Private	30	31
Religious or church-operated	7	7
"Foreign"	9	10
Total	68*	76*

* Totals exceed the number of respondents because some attended more than one type of school.

also needs modification. The religious affiliations of forty-eight respondents are shown below. The number of Protestants was again an overrepresentation, perhaps due to the same cause that distorts the number of

	No.
Catholic	29
Protestant	10
Jewish	2
None	7

women: the fact that the residence foundation mentioned is Protestant. Yet even discounting this distortion, Protestants seem more likely to study in the United States than Catholics, for they constitute only 0.91 per cent of Mexico's population.[3]

Of special interest is the number of nonreligious students. Although nonreligious individuals constitute only 2.26 per cent of the Mexican population, Iturriaga[4] points out that they are mostly middle- and upperclass literate adults and that as a group they have wielded an influence disproportionate to their numbers throughout much of Mexican history.

Those who said that they were Catholic also vary considerably, ranging from individuals who indicated considerable anti-clericalism to others who were emphatically, and one might say belligerently, Catholic. Some devout Catholics were markedly tolerant: one actually attended a Protestant church for a year for the express purpose of learning about Protestantism. At the conclusion of the year he stated that he now understood Protestantism much better and that he was forced to respect Protestants as he respected any persons of high moral standards. At the same

[3] Iturriaga, *op. cit.,* p. 144.
[4] *Ibid.,* pp. 146, 148.

time he was convinced of the rightness of Catholicism, both for himself and for Mexico.

The distribution of students according to field of study, academic status, and post-return goals is given in Table 4. A comparison of these data with the university attended in the United States suggested that considerable selectivity was exercised by the Mexican student in choosing his place of study in this country. Relatively few undergraduates, apparently, attend institutions with large, high-quality graduate schools. Students enrolled in curriculums in the humanities or business were predominantly in undergraduate institutions, while those with teaching and research goals were almost wholly in institutions with large graduate schools.

Table 4. Distribution of Students by Field of Study, Academic Status, and Post-Return Goals

| | Status | | Post-Return Goals | |
Field of Study	Undergraduate	Graduate	Teaching or Research	Business, Professional, or Government
Life science *	2	5	6	1
Physical science	1	2	2	1
Social science	2	4	2	4
Humanities	1	1	2	0
Business	4	1	0	5
Professional	10	2	0	12
Total	20	15	12	23†

* Includes one student each in schools of agriculture, forestry, and medicine who were preparing for research careers.
† An additional eight undergraduates and nine graduates failed to state goals clearly but eleven of these were registered in business or professional curriculums.

Interview materials suggest that this appearance of selectivity is misleading. Mexican students before arrival were familiar with only a relatively small number of United States colleges and universities, and where personal choice was involved, selection was apt to be based upon either the advice of North American friends or foreknowledge gained from previous students at the institutions. One student believed that financially and academically it might be difficult to enter some of the more famous institutions. He therefore obtained the names of several midwestern universities offering work in his special field and wrote to them all. Only one of the institutions replied to his inquiry, and this determined his undergraduate career. After securing the B.A. he made a well-informed selection of an institution for graduate work.

Students under fellowship arrangements, on the other hand, often had little or no choice, and for two of the three interviewed UCLA was a second choice. Some students who might be thought to have scholarly interests because of the undergraduate curriculums they were enrolled in (for example, English literature) said their main objective was to improve their English in order to use it in business.

The prestige of the European university still is high in Mexico, and many students even in professional and technical fields at some time in their career had wished to go to Europe. For example, Enrique Jiménez originally thought European work in his field of interest was best until he began reading technical papers from the United States; this changed his view. But even students who were thoroughly convinced of the superiority of technical training in the United States often felt that a European university would have provided more humanistically oriented training. Students also believed that the older universities of the Atlantic seaboard of the United States provide more humanistically oriented training than do midwestern or western universities.

The bare recital of the facts about the Mexican student may be misleading to the North American reader. To be urban, to be upper middle class, to be Catholic — these characteristics and others have different meanings in Mexico from what they have in the United States. The variant meanings of Catholicism have already been discussed (Chapter 1, pp. 26–27), but a few comments on urbanism and the class designations seem desirable.

Apartment house dwelling and suburbanism are relatively recent phenomena in Mexico for higher class groups. Many students from urban backgrounds had passed part of their lives in old houses owned by their families and, in smaller cities, located near the central plaza. Such houses front directly on the street and are built around a central courtyard. Communication between second-story rooms is along balconies. Commercial activities may occupy the front or all of the lower floor; in any case there is no sharp division of commercial and residential areas. Servants are numerous. Home social activities mainly involve relatives;

restaurants and social athletic clubs are the locus of most other social activities and recreation.

In traditional terms, social status depends in descending order upon family, *educación,* inherited wealth (preferably land), participation in the power structure, and occupation. In newer terms, wealth looms more important as a determiner of social status and other sources of wealth than land are increasingly acceptable. Participation in the power structure gives high status only if accompanied by *educación* and some wealth. Family, while less important, especially in the large urban centers, is still significant. Families with even the most "modern" outlook normally relax supervision of the social life of their children only when the families of the children's companions are well and favorably known. Outstanding achievement in sports, the arts, or politics may gain social acceptance for individuals of lower-class origin but the higher status rarely will extend to their wives or children.

PERSONALITY CHARACTERISTICS OF MEXICAN STUDENTS

The absence of Mexican norms makes it impossible to assert with precision that Mexicans who study in the United States differ in personality characteristics from their peers in Mexico. The main sources for our assessment of psychological characteristics are a Sentence Completion Test (see Appendix) and our interviews with the core group. The data apply to students at the time of our study and do not necessarily indicate anything about their personalities before their United States experience.

Although there is some question as to whether the results of the Sentence Completion Test have the same significance for Mexicans that they have for American subjects, a comparison of the data with interview materials supports the interpretation that individuals making low scores are well adjusted. The top quartile (poorest adjusted) and bottom quartile when compared showed statistically significant differences in some categories of the test and a high degree of similarity in others. In the latter case it may be reasonably assumed that we have discovered fairly common characteristics of the students in our sample.

Most students showed fairly high levels of social adjustment, a conclusion supported by interview materials. Medium to high scores in fear and guilt feelings predominated. However, the actual content of expressions was relatively trivial and tended to center about childhood events or mistakes in practical choices. On the whole, goal and occupa-

41

tional orientations were realistic, although often competitiveness was lacking and the student satisfied with relatively low performance levels. Nevertheless, although the scores suggested that most students had made a good occupational adjustment, some students were diffuse and unrealistic and this was reflected in the scores also — the well adjusted made significantly lower scores as a group than did the poorly adjusted. The majority showed evidence of substantial difficulties in family adjustment, most marked among women, but again the best adjusted group showed significantly less family difficulty than did the poorly adjusted.

One group of responses may be related to authoritarianism in the Mexican social structure. Most students accepted authority and got on well with superiors, associates, and colleagues. In this respect there was no significant difference between the best adjusted and the poorly adjusted. Significantly also the responses concerning colleagues stressed abilities and moral qualities rather than personal relations and personality traits. In attitudes toward people supervised, however, there was a significant difference between the two adjustment groups. Well-adjusted students seemed friendly and tolerant of the people they supervised and willing to accept the role of supervisor. Poorly adjusted students tended either to reject the role of supervisor or to show very harsh and hostile attitudes toward the persons supervised.

In view of the frequent statement by Mexican students that Americans are friendly but their friendships are shallow, Mexican attitudes toward friends are especially interesting. Thirty-seven out of forty-two students responding showed either neutral or markedly hostile attitudes toward their friends. Both personal observation and literary sources show the intimate loyal "best friend," *el amigo íntimo,* to be very important in Mexico but many students thought such friends to be very rare. These attitudes are not incompatible with the nature of Mexican culture and society. The lack of personal loyalties outside the family has been remarked by many observers, both Mexican and foreign. The importance of the extended family and the inclusion of valued outsiders through the *compadre* system tend to inhibit the formation of important affective ties or the development of loyalties to nonrelatives.

The majority of the students showed medium to high confidence in their own abilities and viewed the future in moderately to strongly optimistic terms. Only three students strongly rejected the past or seem to have been markedly unhappy. The majority, if they expressed discontent, dealt either with trivial childhood matters or generalized wishes that they had studied harder, been more serious, and the like. Awareness of the self and perception of social goals was medium to good among almost all students. In all these respects, the most adjusted group showed significantly better scores than the least adjusted group.

The pattern of similarities and differences between the best and poorest adjusted students is congruent with what we know about Mexican culture. In categories where Mexican culture is undergoing change, the poorly adjusted make much poorer scores. In categories where the culture is not undergoing marked change and where no conflicting themes exist, no significant differences appear in the scores of the two groups.

Some individuals varied markedly from the general trends described. In a few instances, none of which happened to be in the interview group, test materials suggested great rigidity and strong generalized hostilities. The career goals of some apparently well-adjusted individuals were sheer fantasies, while others with poor adjustment scores in some areas were dedicated to scholarly careers with which they were quite happy. In effect, they seemed well adjusted to being different.

A few students revealed serious personality problems and adjustment difficulties. Wherever case histories were adequate, these problems seemed to have roots in the period before the student came to the United States. In the most severely disturbed case, the student's loyalty to his family long had been in conflict with his growing consciousness of Mexico's social ills and his acceptance of the revolutionary goals of land reform which threatened his family's wealth. Deeper personality factors were undoubtedly at work, for other students with similar histories were well adjusted. Two other students with personality problems revealed a lifelong history of poor social adjustment and an unusual degree of conflict with their families.

We do not intend to suggest that personal problems were not aggravated by the situation in which the Mexican student found himself in this country. Rather our data suggest that severe personality problems that developed after arrival in the United States already existed in latent or manifest form and were accentuated by the stresses the student encountered. Inadequate as the data are, they suggest that virtually all Mexican students who come to the United States are in some measure atypical or marginal with respect to their cultural and social backgrounds. Interpretations of ideological materials (see the Appendix) as well as interview materials suggest that with very few exceptions students not only considered Mexico to be undergoing change but believed that as individuals they had changed more than the majority of their fellow countrymen. The potentialities for conflict and maladjustment probably are minimized by the fact that not only did most students see themselves as leaders but they did not see themselves as isolated individuals. Rather they felt they were part of a forward-looking segment of the Mexican population. Nevertheless, most students had problems with conflicting values and loyalties. These appeared most frequently in relation to the family and, tentatively, among those identified with the earlier agrarian and ultra-nationalist phase of the Mexican revolution.

In the ideological test, two students indicated strong rejection of both Mexico and the United States. As these students were not in the interview group and the meager background information offers no clues, the meaning of this rejection is not clear. Provisionally, it seems likely that there was a numerically small group of students falling outside our possible generalizations.

TYPES OF INTEREST IN THE UNITED STATES:
GOALS AND MOTIVATIONS

We have established that the Mexican students in our sample came from the urban middle and upper classes. Now we may ask why some people from these groups study in the United States and others do not. The availability of fellowships or funds for private study undoubtedly was a determining factor in some cases. Nevertheless, many Mexicans who could study in the United States clearly do not choose to do so. Discussion of the selective factors which may be at work consequently seems pertinent, although without a control group of persons who chose not to come to the United States, conclusions must be tentative and exploratory.

In this connection the evidence of the ideologies instrument (see the Appendix) seems highly pertinent. Our subjects were asked to check what they considered to be the dominant Mexican ideologies and the dominant United States ideologies, and then to indicate whether they agreed or disagreed with each. Overwhelmingly we found that our subjects tended to disagree with their own estimate of dominant Mexican ideologies. Mean scores for the group showed only 77 per cent agreement. The agreement score for one student was 100 per cent, but the remainder ranged downward to as low as 27 per cent. Although the picture is less clear, those who disagreed most with their estimates of Mexican ideologies tended to agree with their estimates of United States ideologies. There were notable exceptions to this pattern, however, and some individuals who tended strongly to disagree with their estimate of Mexican ideology also disagreed with their estimate of United States ideology. On the other hand, the five students who indicated highest agreement with their estimate of Mexican ideology also indicated high agreement with their estimate of United States ideology. In other words, they minimized differences between the two cultures. Four of these students were in professional, technical, and business fields, and two out of the five planned to remain in the United States.

When the ideologies test results were analyzed for the students' agreement with traditional values, the trend of disagreement was clear. With almost no exceptions, the Mexican students considered themselves less traditional in their ideas than the bulk of their fellow countrymen. The interview materials suggest strongly that this self-image was viewed as "liberal" or "progressive." They believed that Mexico is in an era of economic and social change and that they were or would become leaders in such change. Generally speaking, they had rejected the traditional view of a static society and had embraced the idea of progress.

Finally, it seems fairly clear that the motivations for United States study for the majority of the students were related to a sense of social obligation. It may well be — although empirical evidence is scanty — that Mexican students in the United States were more socially oriented and less individualistic than the average Mexican is. Most students were in some degree motivated by a desire to do something for Mexico and for not a few this was the major motivation for foreign study.

Social motivations were perhaps weakest in those students who came to the United States primarily to improve their English for use in business. Even these, however, were usually attempting to learn additional business skills, and many believed that the application of improved techniques in business and industry would help to solve Mexico's social and economic problems.

Social motivations were strongest among students studying in fields where they believed their personal careers might possibly be hampered by prejudice against Mexicans trained in the United States. They believed the training and skills they sought in the United States would be beneficial for Mexico and hoped in time to receive recognition. While all students probably expect some ultimate personal advantage as a result of study in the United States, this group believed they had foregone rapid and easy success in order to further long range and socially useful goals.

The characterization of most Mexican students as liberal, progressive, or nontraditional needs some qualification. Thus far the discussion has been in terms of the over-all patterns presented by each student. When categories of ideology were examined it became clear that for most students the rejection of traditional positions was selective.

Compared with believers in traditional Mexican ideologies, students tended to (1) be less authoritarian (but with some striking exceptions); (2) favor greater social equality for women (rejected by the most traditionally oriented students); (3) favor more liberal child-rearing practices; (4) believe more in knowledge (especially science) as an instrument of human welfare; (5) be less individualistic (although strongly favoring individual freedom); (6) believe more in democracy and a changing or dynamic society.

Retention of some aspects of traditional Mexican ideology was suggested by the fact that students tended to (1) emphasize the importance of the family; (2) support humanistic and spiritual values as opposed to materialistic values; (3) retain (often unconsciously) strong class attitudes and values (a contradiction of (6) above).

It is quite possible, in the absence of any control data, that the characteristics enumerated above may be common to university students in Mexico as well as those who study in the United States. If that is true the data do not help us to understand why particular students come to this country. Nevertheless, they do suggest areas of ideological conflict for the students and have some bearing on the problems of readjustment after return, for one may safely assume that the more traditionally oriented critics of returned students will be quick to link nontraditional attitudes with study in the United States whenever possible.

In addition to the possible effect of the rejection of some aspects of traditional ideology on the decision of Mexican students to study in the United States, there are other factors that may exert an influence. Among such factors may be attendance at "foreign" secondary schools such as the American School in Mexico City, the experiences of relatives and friends who have studied in the United States, and contacts with Americans in Mexico. Coupled with these is an acceptance of the technological superiority of the United States and a belief either that better training may be secured in this country or that study here will be a valuable supplement or extension of training already received.

Most students felt that improvement of understanding between the two nations was a product of student exchange but, with one doubtful exception, this was not a personal goal. Those who expressed opinions were emphatic in their belief that student exchange is the best way to improve understanding between nations and that an expansion of exchange is therefore desirable. On the other hand, understanding was not seen as the proper direct objective of an exchange program. Rather, it was regarded as a by-product of programs designed to meet the needs of the students.

KNOWLEDGE AND PRECONCEPTIONS ABOUT THE UNITED STATES

Preconceptions of the United States played an important part in determining the ease and rapidity of the Mexican student's adjustment to this country. The formation of such preconceptions is undoubtedly a complex process, involving among other things the amount and accuracy of the student's information about the United States, the conscious and unconscious prejudices and biases of the student and of his sources of information, the student's critical ability, and perhaps rather importantly his ability to convert essentially symbolic and scattered information and impressions into an integrated pattern and imaginatively to endow it with reality. If the student's preconceptions approximate what he encounters, in a sense he has made a prior adjustment; to the extent that his expectations are not met, his adjustment may be more difficult than if he were totally ignorant.

In only a few cases was it possible to interview students within a short time after their arrival in the United States. Most of the data are thus retrospective, but even after several years students retained vivid impressions of the significant ways in which their experiences in the United States conformed to or contradicted their preconceptions. Some indirect material may be gleaned from the instruments. Personal experience of the authors in Mexico and familiarity with Mexican literature and mass media provide subjective corroboration.

Understanding of the preconceptions of the Mexican student before he has come to the United States requires recognition of a fact seldom realized by the North American. If one can probe deeply enough below the heavy armor of courtesy, virtually every Mexican reveals a significant amount of anti-American feeling. This is true not only before he comes to the United States; it is true while he is here and it remains true after he returns. Nevertheless, such a statement requires analysis, and changes while the student is in the United States, and after his return.

Even the form of this broad preliminary assertion is repugnant to most Mexicans, for the Mexican regards himself as an American. He resents the usurpation of the term American by the United States and by United States citizens. To him we are North Americans or "United Statesans," to use a form possible in Spanish but horrid in English; or we are *yanquis* or gringos, often unprintably qualified, depending upon his sentiments at the moment.

The North American — meaning the citizen of the United States — with his strong desire to be liked, may find these sweeping statements shocking and in some measure bewildering. Yet, if he knew Mexican history as well as Mexicans do, he would not be surprised. To a Mexican the United States is a country which has persistently interfered in the affairs of Mexico. This he learns in primary school — if he attends one, he reads in his newspapers and magazines, he hears mentioned in innumerable conversations. On three occasions Mexican soil has been invaded by United States troops, the last two times within the memory of many Mexicans now living. By force of arms the United States took from Mexico more than half its territory — although some Mexicans blame this upon General Santa Ana rather than upon the United States. Under Díaz, United States business firms received great privileges, and at that period and later were, in the opinion of most Mexicans, guilty of great exploitation. Even today United States corporations operating in Mexico are believed to pay Mexican employees but a half or a third of what they pay North Americans doing the same work. North American capital is generally believed to be devoted to the exploitation of Mexican raw materials rather than to enterprises strengthening the Mexican economic structure. In the struggle for political and economic independence that followed the 1910 revolution, many Mexicans saw the United States as doing its best to interfere with the processes of the revolution, interference leading perilously close to war in the period immediately before the appointment of Ambassador Dwight Morrow in 1927. And the Mexican has seen his country invaded by hundreds of thousands of tourists for whose patronage and dollars he is grateful, yet who, in many cases, conduct themselves in ways that humiliate the Mexican.

If this were not enough, the Mexican has also seen the United States take part in both armed and unarmed intervention in the affairs of other Latin American countries, he has seen what he considers economic imperialism at work in many areas, he knows that the United States is rich and militarily powerful and Mexico poor and relatively weak. If he is a thoughtful person at all he knows that so long as this condition continues — and he is realistic enough to recognize that it may continue indefinitely — Mexico is not a free agent in many areas of international affairs. Indeed, the surprising thing is not that Mexicans are anti-American, but that they are not more strongly so.

While it is true that virtually all Mexicans are anti-American, important qualifications of the statement are necessary. The generalized hostility does not mean that any particular citizen of the United States is automatically disliked. In the first place Mexicans tend to judge the North Americans they know on the basis of individual behavior rather than by stereotypes. It is entirely possible for a person from the United States to pass many years in Mexico without a single serious inconvenience or disagreeable experience attributable to anti-American feeling. Further, as his sophistication increases, the Mexican begins to distinguish among government, business, and the individual American. This is particularly true of students coming to the United States, who not only tend to make this distinction, but increasingly recognize that even government and business have, from their point of view, both good and bad aspects. It will be apparent, we believe, that although the student who comes to the United States rarely becomes an uncritical and wholehearted supporter of the United States in every respect, he does grow in understanding and discrimination and usually finds many things about the United States which he approves.

It has already been made clear that most of the Mexican students in our study would have preferred to go to Europe to study. Only the students primarily concerned with technology, in medicine or business or industry or some special scientific fields, had come to the United States by preference. To understand this we must examine the preconceptions and their sources.

Mexican students as a whole are probably more fully and accurately informed about the United States before their arrival than are most foreign students. Mexican newspapers, especially in Mexico City, carry a considerable amount of United States news, including news from the major wire services. Many of our students had read a great deal about the United States, both critical books and magazine treatments, and had read some United States literature. Many had met Americans in Mexico and had friends, relatives, and acquaintances who had traveled or studied in the United States. In the regions from which most students came, possibly as many as one in five adults have been in the United States. In many cases the students themselves had traveled in the United States before coming here to study. A fair proportion of the students had attended an American school (see Table 2). All had seen many American motion pictures. Because they knew that the Mexican motion pictures give a distorted account of life in Mexico, they tended to believe that American movies distort life in the United States in the same way, but nevertheless American movies familiarized them with many of the objective aspects of American life.

As a result of such knowledge and experience, the Mexican students usually had modified their basic anti-American sentiments before arrival. The majority were critical but not unfriendly. They were familiar with the more obvious life ways in this country and anticipated the material aspects of life here. In the more intangible aspects of life, they were less well prepared.

On the whole the Mexican students presented a fairly uniform set of preconceptions. Before arrival, they believed the United States to be rich and highly mechanized; to have a high standard of living, large cities, big buildings, and a rush of traffic. Perhaps even more than do most Latin Americans or Asians, the Mexican student considered the United States to have a materialistic society with little regard for humanistic values, for music, art, literature, or indeed any sense of the true meaning of life. Predominantly, although a student might know of exceptions, he believed that a citizen of the United States was concerned with gaining money and material goods. As a crass people we were believed lacking in manners, to have no family life, our children to be undisciplined, and divorce to be a commonplace. American men do not love their wives, the Mexicans felt, because they let them do as they please. The freedom of women and girls was thought to mean sexual immorality. To the Mexican Catholic, the United States is a Protestant country, peopled by followers of religious ideas he has been taught to abhor. But even these we do not really put into practice, and hence the United States is believed to be an irreligious country.

With such a picture, one may ask why our Mexican students came to the United States. Some, it is true, came only for the technical skills they hoped to acquire. Others had found reason to modify their opinions or had contradictory images of some significance. Those interested in the industrialization of Mexico did not see American business and industry as wholly evil. Some had worked for American corporations and saw in use there management skills they might acquire. The more widely read and thoughtful were also aware that out of the United States, from time to time, have emerged important political ideals. Even though they might feel that the United States believes in democracy only within its own borders, they often recognized the effectiveness of American political democracy. Some recognition of these ideas goes far back in time, and many Mexicans are aware of the indebtedness of the founders of Mexican independence to the American Revolution and to the formulators of the United States Constitution. In more modern times individuals have found expressions of great significance in the proclamation of the Four Freedoms, the idealism felt to be inherent in the Marshall Plan, and the support of the United Nations.

Let us examine the statements of students of our core group. Said Gonzalo Reyes: "First my impressions of the United States were against it, since I began reading all the Spanish philosophers: Ortega y Gasset. . . . So the impression we had was that the United States did not care very much about art or the people that really count. I believed that Americans did not teach anything about living, being phlegmatic, practical, not sentimental, and not having poetry. . . . Of course, afterwards this changed when I began reading other things. James could be convincing, and Dewey also. But even at that it's very cold, being pragmatic and in terms of action, being practical in life, that is about business, not caring much about your wife, letting her do anything. And then there was imperialism — just for business; going over and taking our land, taking over Venezuela, and Nicaragua, and all that — the bananas and coconuts and oil."

On another occasion Gonzalo referred to his attitudes during World War II when he was a student at the University of Mexico. Then he felt the war to be one among imperialists. "Actually there were some who liked the Japanese, not the Nazis, but the Japanese, because the hatred against . . . not really hatred, but . . . there is that thing about United States imperialism, there is always a certain feeling against the United

States. And when the Japanese bombarded Pearl Harbor, well, we couldn't feel that the United States . . . we didn't have anything to do with the war, nothing to go to war for. Besides we were suffering poverty without having to go to war." And speaking of student attitudes in various places in Mexico, he felt that as a group, "we felt opposed to the United States because of its imperialistic history . . . we thought it was imperialistic . . . we still think it was in some ways. What we didn't like was the way that they were making propaganda, saying that Mexico, a naturally rich country, was being wasted because of bad government, and the people were lazy . . . so we had to dislike the United States for the way they were treating us, saying the Mexicans were childish. Perhaps we were, but in some ways we believed in something and were trying to prepare. And, again, we thought that we weren't being treated fairly, we were being abused by the superiority complex of the imperialistic United States."

There were some things, of course, that Gonzalo liked. "We liked the women, they were all very pretty . . . we had the impression that the American girls were easy. It isn't true, but we thought so."

Less hostile and better informed was Roberto Rosales, whose father had studied at Berkeley, whose brother and sister had traveled in the United States, whose fiancée had studied in Boston, who knew American families residing in his home town, and who had been employed for a few months by an American corporation. He had a long-standing interest in coming to the United States, and a good many technical objectives. He pointed out that American films were not representative of American life, although he did feel that from films one could deduce that the psychology of the American people is much more simple than that of Latin Americans. He had an impression that Americans were easier to get on with than Latin Americans, although there was less respect in the relations between girls and boys. Nevertheless, he felt that "in the United States there exists a great liberty which is often converted into excess, an excess beyond that which is moral."

Enrique Jiménez likewise had few antagonisms toward the United States by the time he arrived, although his earlier impressions were more favorable toward Europe. He thought of the United States "as a big country with civilized people; all of them, or at least most of them, having a high standard of living with facilities for living well and making good work. . . . I knew that even the worker of the factory has his own car and his refrigerator, and all the things that make for comfortable living, which in

Mexico our laborers don't have." He was aware of the productive capacity of the United States, its efficient methods of organization, and ability to supply most material needs. He was not particularly interested in American music or other aspects of American life, although he preferred American movies to Mexican movies.

Enrique came to the United States for specialized medical training. As he remarked, "I didn't look forward to social activities." He felt that doctors were respected in the United States much more than in Mexico, and he felt that "on the higher intellectual levels there is not discrimination; people are cultivated — not only those who have a higher degree — just people who have traveled, for instance, who have a culture and a certain opinion about all the world." Basically, however, Enrique had few interests in United States politics or society.

Isabella Lopez, on the other hand, had definite anti-American prejudices. She had no contacts with American ideas in grammar school, which was an English school using Canadian textbooks. In the afternoons she had Mexican history and accounts of wars with the United States, "so I guess that was the first impression I had." She met some American girls casually, but they added to her prejudice. Isabella considers her attitudes rather puritanical, but "all American girls were quite fresh. They started going out with boys when they were very young, and kissing and necking all the time. That's what my friends' idea of American girls is." Some of her impressions were from movies, some from talking with Mexican girls who had visited in the United States. An uncle had also given her some prejudices against the United States.

The above description of the hostile attitudes and unfavorable images would seem to be contradicted by the presence of fairly large numbers of Mexican students studying in United States universities without financial aids or inducements. We have already implied that many of the students coming to the United States have undergone some favorable modification in their attitudes and preconceptions. Nevertheless some students were (and remain) strongly nationalistic, anti-American, belligerently Catholic, and overtly hostile both to the United States and to American culture. Such extreme cases call for some explanation.

All our evidence suggests that the common motivation which will overrule all others is the student's belief either that he can secure better training in his field in the United States or that he will profit by supplementary training in his field. Training in professional, technical, and scientific fields is the aspect of United States culture which the Mexican is most apt to concede to be valuable or superior to Mexican culture. Hence opportunities for such training may bring to this country even the most nationalistic, anti-American, and traditional Catholics. The most hostile and aggressive subject in the noninterview group, who took pains to emphasize his devout Catholicism, and who saw nothing else good in the United States, nevertheless considered his professors here "magnificent" and his year of special training excellent.

Yet despite exceptions, our data suggest that in general students who are strongly anti-American, what the Mexicans would call "fanatic" Catholics, and who are traditionally oriented will rarely study in the United States. Nationalistic and anti-American students who are not traditionally oriented and who are less fervently committed to Catholicism are more apt to study in the United States. The majority, however, will have tempered or suppressed their hostile feelings toward the United States as a result of experience, business relationships, or family connections. Students with no prior history of hostility toward the United States will be very few and there will be quite non-typical facts in their life histories, such as Protestant parents, training, and education, or they will be very narrowly dedicated to technical or research goals.

3

Adaptation to United States Life

IN THIS chapter we will discuss some of the experiences of the Mexican student as he moves from his own culture to the United States. Among topics to be considered are the first impressions and the degree to which they conformed to expectations, the problems of organizing personal life in terms of living conditions and social relationships, the kinds of adjustments achieved and the extent to which they were satisfactory, and the evaluation of the academic and living experience. In the next chapter we will consider opinions and attitudes in selected areas and their stability or change while in this country.

The data on adaptation and adjustment come mainly from the small interview group at UCLA and are not necessarily representative. They are, moreover, retrospective, the recall of events and situations often several years in the past. On the other hand, a variety of experiences are represented and the information at least suggests consistent patterns. Moreover, many experiences remain vivid memories, although we recognize that vividness is no guarantee of accuracy of recall, especially at affective levels. Retrospective accounts by returned students interviewed in Mexico are strikingly similar.

FIRST IMPRESSIONS

In the previous chapter, the discussion of sources of information and preconceptions suggests that at the objective external level Mexican students are well prepared for the life they will encounter in the United States. Thus large cities, heavy traffic, crowds, great activity, greater wealth, and less obvious poverty were all expected. It is true that New York skyscrapers for some appeared larger than they had expected. But students long conditioned to the frenetic activity of the central section of Mexico City, one of the larger cities of the hemisphere, in some cases found the hurry, bustle, and confusion less than they had expected. Some even suggest that the stereotype of the hardworking American, always in a hurry, is a myth.

Of downtown Los Angeles one student says: "All I see there is big buildings; people rushing to the corner to stop on a red light, rushing on a green light; lots of business; poor people walking and talking to themselves, lots of drunkards — Main Street — burlesque shows; just like my city — like the downtown area of Mexico City." Asked to compare New York, Los Angeles, Mexico City, and Monterrey he said: "Somehow here the standard of living does do something to the social behavior, but there is the same individualism in all of them, the same going towards your own job; with the carrying on of friendships and doing things that will be good for you and your friends, forgetting the bad things happening around; going to a bus you try to get there first."

The greater cleanliness and orderliness of American cities was commented upon by several. One woman student at UCLA was so struck by the difference in the way automobile traffic is regulated that she confessed to crossing Wilshire Boulevard a number of times just for the pleasure of seeing the automobiles stop for her. At the risk of being accused of local chauvinism, it may be observed that perhaps because of their rarity (and because of stricter law enforcement?) pedestrians receive consideration from motorists in Los Angeles to a degree hardly credible to a resident of New York or Chicago, and even more astonishing to a resident of Mexico City.

Housing difficulties apparently did not exceed expectations; most students felt that their greatest difficulties stemmed from insufficient money. Especially in the Los Angeles area, distances exceeded expectations and transportation problems were vexatious. American food seemed uninspired; "insipid" was a word used more than once.

Although no students interviewed were from border towns, we may surmise that the first impressions of such students would be different in some cases. They would, for example, already be familiar with American food, but those from such a town as Piedras Negras probably would undergo experiences similar to an American student's when he first visits a large city.

Of more significance than first impressions in objective and physical aspects of life are experiences in personal and social relationships. However much the individual is prepared for new living conditions, he must approach life among an alien people with some apprehension. This apprehension may be slightly diminished if he has known Americans in his home country, but there remains in his mind the question of how typical these Americans were. The behavior of persons in authority; the practices of ticket offices, stores, and restaurants, and the actions, speech, and manner of their personnel; and the pattern of manners toward the stranger — all are difficult to anticipate and visualize. If first impressions are important in coloring subsequent adjustment — a reasonable hypothesis certainly — then initial contacts with Americans in their home country are significant.

The interview group clearly came to the United States with a measure of favorable disposition but also with the expectation that they would have some uncomfortable if not unpleasant experiences. It is likely that this was true of a very large majority of the Mexican students. Most students interviewed had in fact undergone unpleasant or inconvenient experiences early in their visit to the United States. Probably a majority felt unnecessarily inconvenienced by or sensed hostility from immigration or customs officials or both. Others had early had unpleasant experiences with individual Americans.

The students' accounts of these experiences suggest that only if they had sensed a recurring pattern in these experiences would their attitudes have been affected noticeably. They tended to identify unpleasant or hostile experiences with officials as characteristic of bureaucracy and cited similar experiences at home. Individuals who were unpleasant were correctly identified as unpleasant individuals rather than as typical Americans. Even students who had had the worst experiences — or felt the greatest resentment — were quick to counter these with stories of pleasant experiences. If no pleasant experiences intervene, it is probable that a newcomer will construe unpleasant experiences as characteristic and form generalized unfavorable judgments. In the interview group, however, the initial judgments of all were that, despite any unpleasant experiences, Americans on the whole are more courteous and friendly than they had expected. A few noted greater informality of personal relationships among Americans; the men usually approved this but the women were affronted at first.

Juan Ortega's "mixed" experiences are perhaps typical. In his home town the United States consul told him it would be impossible to give him a visa in time for him to arrive here for the opening of school. Juan felt that the consul's manner was antagonistic and cavalier. A secretary then intervened and worked until nine in the evening to complete the necessary documents. Thus his first impression was mixed. When he arrived at the border, the customs men were thorough and disagreeable. But at the bus station, where he had difficulty because of his faulty English, a sailor who spoke some Spanish heard him mention his destination, asked if he were going to the university, bought his ticket, and gave him addresses of cheap rooming houses and the names of friends. "He was very, very charming, very, very, helpful . . . that would be a little bit difficult to happen in Latin America. That was very warming." (And for the record, this same kind of thing could easily happen to an American traveling in Latin America.)

On the bus he sensed that a man was talking about him and making people laugh at him. On the other hand the man sitting next to him tried to distract his attention from the others. The bus driver carried him past his destination, but then to his surprise gave him a free ticket back. At the university, the foreign student adviser was cordial, placed him in a dormitory, and introduced him to a group of American students who were very friendly and took him to the coffee shop. There someone passing the table said in Spanish, "How many ugly people come to this University."

Juan cited a number of other such contrasting examples, for he had spent more time in the United States than any other student. Obviously the unpleasant experiences had affected him rather deeply, for he was both sensitive and anxious to be liked. But he always dwelt at length on the many people who had done helpful things for him and the close friendships he had made. Clearly he did not think Americans as a whole are unpleasant. Rather, from his total life story it is evident that he had met a fair number of unpleasant people and some of these happened to be Americans. In addition, although he did not say so explicitly, he conveyed the impression that he thought some Americans were unpleasant to him because he was a foreigner.

In contrast, Enrique Jiménez on his first trip to the United States (except for a few days in New York while returning from Europe) traveled by bus halfway across the country. In a Texas bus station people were not polite to him but in the "North" people were very nice and he felt accepted. When he came to the United States to study, his plane was held several hours at the border by the authorities. He assumed the delay involved bureaucratic harassment of Mexican passengers but as he was able to spend this time talking to an attractive Mexican movie actress, he was not vexed by it. He admitted no other disagreeable experiences, and early in the school year decided he would not be disillusioned about the United States. Everything was as he imagined and he was happy.

Several students at UCLA reported dissatisfaction on arrival with the behavior of clerical personnel in administrative offices. These problems are elaborated in Chapter 4.

In summary, students found physical conditions and living problems not greatly different from their expectations. While the relatively greater orderliness of American cities impressed some, others saw big cities as basically much alike with similar virtues and drawbacks. Problems of housing, adjusting to a new diet, and learning one's way about were vexatious but within the range of expectation. In social and personal contacts, some found both government and university bureaucrats at times frustrating and irritating but, in the worst incidents reported, other bureaucrats came to the student's aid. Individual Americans were disagreeable to some students, but on the whole they were more courteous and friendly than the students had expected. Most students, and especially those reporting unpleasant incidents, took pains to report cases of unusual helpfulness on the part of faculty, students, or even casual strangers.

The written instruments suggest some students of the larger group of students in our sample who were not interviewed had high levels of hostility or rejection toward the United States. It is possible that such students would report less favorable first impressions but unfortunately no extreme cases occurred among the students interviewed.

INITIAL ADJUSTMENT PROBLEMS

Other studies suggest that foreign students tend to pass through a series of adjustment periods. In the initial "spectator" phase they are detached observers with a minimum of involvement. After a period varying in length with individuals, an "involvement" phase begins. Adjustment problems increase, frustrations are experienced, opinions and images are found false or subject to modification. The students' morale declines and their opinions of the United States and the university become less favorable. If students are here long enough, they pass through this adaptive phase, and enter a "coming-to-terms" phase. If the adjustment is positive, associations with Americans increase and usually morale and attitudes improve. In some cases adjustment may consist of withdrawal and immersion in studies. In other cases, a more objective but neutral equilibrium may be attained. For a few, the equilibrium may be charged with negative affect accompanied by free expression of overt criticisms and verbal aggressiveness. Finally, shortly before the return to the home country, a second decline may occur as the student begins to worry about his acceptance and adjustment at home. He tends to relieve his apprehensions by finding fault with the United States and the university. Both in the timing of these phases and in the style of adjustment there are many individual and national differences.

We have no reason to believe that Mexican students' adjustment patterns are different from those of other foreign students. But the smallness of our samples, the differences in prior knowledge, and the varying length of stay in the United States make it impossible to document such patterns positively for the Mexican students. Such relevant information as we have, however, suggests that Mexican students do pass through similar phases and exhibit much the same range of individual variation in the timing of the phases and in the modes of adjustment.

The greatest initial adjustment problem of the Mexican student unquestionably is linguistic. This would be less true of students from border states or with extensive education in American language preparatory schools. Students on government scholarships also have somewhat less trouble, an evidence of the effectiveness of the screening of fellowship students. But the majority who are self-supported or family-supported clearly have overestimated their competence in English. Some, indeed, have virtually no English on arrival.

Several students said they did not wish to associate with other Latin American students because they felt this interfered with learning English. These students reported that students from other Latin American countries often criticize or dislike Mexican students. If the student has difficulty forming satisfactory associations with American students, as is usually the case, he then associates with foreign students who do not speak Spanish. In several cases Mexican students roomed with other foreign students but at UCLA we have no case of a Mexican student rooming with a Spanish-speaking student (except for a married couple). Significantly, despite the small number of Mexican nationals at UCLA, no one student knew all the others. In contrast to Indian and Japanese student communities, no Mexican student subculture exists. From fragmentary evidence, we believe this to be the case at other universities also.

Juan Ortega probably had the most difficulty with English, and had the first university he attended employed adequate screening techniques he would certainly have been refused admission. He realized he was failing his courses: "No matter how much I tried to study I always was behind, and even if I read it, that didn't mean that I understood the lecture or the lesson. That was horrible. Well, one night I just cried, I was so frustrated, I just cried. The next day I had an exam; I had been studying till two o'clock in the morning every day, and still I knew already I was going to flunk the exam."

Juan pointed out that his inadequacy in English not only created academic difficulties but was the cause of loneliness. "I couldn't communicate very well with American students, and even if I could communicate, I knew that they wouldn't give a hoot about me and I didn't about them; I mean there was not rapport, and it was very frustrating too."

The university Juan first attended had no special English classes for foreign students. He failed the regular English class three times before a special arrangement was made for him. A faculty adviser took an interest in him and gave him special coaching. Ultimately he obtained a B.A. and became a successful graduate student. Later the university he had attended provided special English classes and Juan reported that his younger brother, arriving with a similar language problem, made a much more rapid adjustment.

Although language difficulties contribute to the isolation of the Mexican students, they experience little difficulty in making social adjustments when they have the opportunity. They exhibited some irritation with naive and ignorant remarks or questions about Mexico. At times they felt people were interested in them as curiosities or famous lovers. "Sometimes I found I was a strange person and they wanted to know someone from a foreign land and I was an odd character. Other people were interested, not because I had something of the exotic because I was a foreigner, but they took me as they would take any other person with whom they wanted to be friends."

Nevertheless, students quickly and easily adjusted to the everyday personal and group interaction situations. Compared with Japanese and Indian students, most Mexican students became very quickly better adjusted socially than most Japanese and Indian students ever become.[1] Aside from lesser linguistic skills, the Mexican social adjustment seemed as easy and almost as complete as that described in an earlier cross-cultural volume for Scandinavian students.[2] Several students reported the early formation of close friendships.

The main area of difficulty, as with other groups, was in relations with the opposite sex. Men, even after several years in the United States, still found themselves baffled by the behavior and attitudes of American girls, particularly with respect to dating patterns and casual affectionate responses. A kiss or even holding hands is, to the Mexican, part of a serious courtship or an invitation to sexual relations. When neither comes about, the Mexican male is wounded in a most sensitive part of his ego, the spot where honor, *egoismo*, and *machismo* are all involved. Comments by American men that they too did not understand American women seemed to relieve these tensions.

Some women students arrived with an idea that American boys would make good husbands. At first they were affronted by the lack of formality in American boys' treatment of them. Once they understood that this did not mean lack of respect, they lost their resentment. They felt, however, that American boys are too much concerned with status (fraternity members especially), with making money, and with having a "good time." To some extent at least, women students, even though they claimed ample opportunities to go out with American boys, apparently began to prefer other foreign students because they were both more serious and more apt to observe the formal courtesies.

American girls were not understood at first by Mexican women students and they remained confusing because they conformed to no single pattern. "They play with boys and they act like another boy when they are with boys, and besides, in their conversation — we take very much care about talking about sexual things among boys, as a matter of fact, we never talk about things like that when we are together but here they don't mind it. I had a very profound conversation with a boy here about that

[1] This opinion is derived from discussions with John W. Bennett and Richard D. Lambert regarding the problems of Japanese and Indian students respectively. The results of the research on Japanese students is in manuscript; the results of the research on Indian students is contained in Richard D. Lambert and Marvin Bressler, *Indian Students on an American Campus* (Minneapolis: University of Minnesota Press, 1956).

[2] Franklin D. Scott, *The American Experience of Swedish Students* (Minneapolis: University of Minnesota Press, 1956).

topic." But some things were good: "They are more free, and on the other hand, I think they are more confident, too, and they can develop their personalities better than we can."

Adjustment to the physical problems of living seemed easy. Difficulties in housing were primarily economic and, like the American students at UCLA, Mexican students were scattered and often lived a long way from the campus. One married couple was refused an apartment when the landlord found they were Mexican, but no similar case was reported. Some who could afford it shared apartments either with other foreign or with American students, especially after their first semester. Others had rooms at various distances from the campus. Several did some of their own cooking but most, especially the men, ate in restaurants. Some at UCLA had lived in co-op dormitories or fraternity houses but none were doing so at the time of the study. At other institutions, the housing situation appeared similar.

American food was believed healthful but tasteless. Most expressed interest in learning where Mexican food could be obtained, but with few exceptions they rarely traveled the extra distance necessary to get it.

At UCLA most students felt hampered by the lack of cars and to some extent by lack of money. Both factors limited their recreational activities and use of cultural opportunities. None seemed much interested in television or radio, even though several Mexican stations can be heard in Los Angeles. Movies were perhaps their major recreation, but most students were selective and critical about them. Free noon concerts on campus were attended by a few. Dances and other recreational events sponsored by campus groups were attended but not systematically and mainly by first-year students. Far from criticizing American night club life, some with money sampled it extensively. "I went to a place last Saturday night on Sunset [a well-known night club on the "Strip"]. There I was impressed. I don't think ever in my life have I even seen such a gathering of beautiful women. And I did try hard enough to look for some that were not good looking — but no, all of them were pretty." Graduate students seemed to enter fairly soon into the social activities of their American fellow graduate students. Two first-year students went on trips to the Grand Canyon and a sponsored tour of the state; they also mentioned parties to which they had been invited by American students. Social and recreational activities, satisfactory or not, were certainly not lacking.

Students not interviewed may have had less satisfactory experiences.

One who returned a questionnaire wrote bitterly and at some length about wasting money on our research instead of doing something to overcome the terrible loneliness of the foreign students.

The sensitive areas found to be so important with, for example, Indian students, seemed of little importance to the Mexican student.[3] The Mexican student was sheltered by two things. In the first place, his belief in the superiority of Mexican culture for its greater emphasis on spiritual and humanistic values and closer family life provided him with a more effective defense than seems the case with Indian students. Second, apparently the most irritating questions such as "Do you have telephones in Mexico?" or statements that "of course all Mexicans are lazy" are met to some extent by the anti-materialistic defenses, and are so manifestly untrue that the Mexican student was annoyed but not driven to further defenses beyond deploring American ignorance. How the Mexican would react to systematic hostile probing on such subjects as *machismo* and the double sex standard, the *mordida* (governmental graft), the pre-Reformation character of the Mexican Catholic Church, the class structure, and the treatment of the Indian, we did not attempt to discover. But so few Americans are sufficiently informed about Mexico to ask questions about these subjects that "sensitive area" reactions here seemed nonexistent.

Only if they have relatives in the United States did Mexican students associate much with Mexican-Americans. Those who met a few Mexican-Americans on the campus at UCLA thought they lacked self-confidence. In general, they felt that Mexican-Americans come from social strata with which they would not associate at home. Although they knew of discrimination against Mexican-Americans, they did not really experience it themselves, and identified it with class discrimination against the same people at home. One who experienced discrimination in Texas dismissed it by saying he considered anyone who practiced discrimination to be an inferior type.

MAINTENANCE OF HOME TIES

Mexican students appeared to make no special efforts to maintain contacts with their home culture. Although Mexican motion pictures are shown regularly at a theater a mile or so from the campus, apparently none

[3] Richard D. Lambert and Marvin Bressler, "The Sensitive Area Complex: A Contribution to the Theory of Guided Culture Contact," *American Journal of Sociology*, 60:583–92 (May 1955).

of our interviewees at UCLA ever attended. Few read Mexican newspapers or periodicals at all systematically nor did they write numerous letters to friends and associates. "Sometimes I buy a card and put on an address and say 'hello.' That's all." On the other hand they wrote regularly and frequently to their families and evinced strong family interests. Parents, especially mothers, exercised important controls even over male students. One male student remarked that of course he would go home immediately if his mother asked him to. He added that she would never ask him to come home unless the need was very great. Ties with siblings often were strong. Another student, married and partially self-supporting, helped a younger brother surreptitiously by giving him part of the money sent by his father, although instructed by his father not to do so.

This appearance of low involvement with the home country and home groups is deceptive. In several cases, students were visited by relatives, usually their mothers, at the mid-year recess or in the summer. Several had relatives in the United States whom they visited or who visited them. Most of those who had been here two years or more had paid visits to Mexico; some spent their summer holidays at home.

Involvement with the home country hence remained high even though overt expression or action was slight. Involvement with the host country on the other hand was low. Although adjustment may be rapid in some cases, Mexican students seem to retain some aspects of the "spectator" orientation even after several years. Few appear even to consider the possibility of remaining in the United States.

Although numbers were too few to allow extensive generalizations, variation in individual styles was evident. Some students seemed to feel little need of supportive relationships beyond those of the home ties with their families. One student, in his third year in the United States, had few friendships or other involvements here although he seemed happy with his studies and manner of life. He was a self-contained, quiet individual with adequate inner resources. His life history suggested that even at home he had only limited involvements, although those he reported seemed warm and normal.

On the other hand, students here for some time, especially at the graduate level, often formed many personal involvements with fellow graduate students. One student married an American wife. Another, a woman, originally hostile toward the United States, after three years underwent a series of very traumatic experiences. Her husband died after a prolonged illness as the result of injuries received in an automobile accident in Mexico. At about the same time her parents were divorced. The strong emotional ties with the friends she had made in the United States made her return to Mexico difficult. She has since revisited the United States and friends from this country visit her in Mexico frequently.

The high permeability of the border, then, was a factor in the maintenance of home ties. None of the core group contemplated permanent residence in the United States. The scanty data for the group that was not interviewed suggest that only those with several family members already living permanently in the United States considered remaining in this country. On the other hand, many obviously felt that by returning to Mexico they would not sever all ties with the United States. They often contemplated return visits to this country. They also looked forward to visits by friends from the United States. Hence most felt that whatever involvements they might have with the United States were not transitory but would continue after return.

To summarize this section in cultural terms, we may say that within a relatively short time the Mexican students learned the overt culture surprisingly well. Particularly, they learned how to utilize the material culture. Adjustment to the social structure of the university took somewhat longer. They learned the culture of students soon but they were often unaware of or took a long time to learn, for example, the culture of the working or business classes. Students early learned to operate within and manipulate their immediate socio-cultural environment. They soon made discriminatory evaluations of segments of both the immediate environment and the larger culture so far as they knew it. Personal involvement with the culture, however, often remained low even for well-adjusted and well-adapted individuals if they were in the United States only a short time. Where personal involvement occurred, it was related on the one hand to the formation of friendships and other social relationships, and on the other to selective comparison of aspects of the new culture with their own. Approval of United States culture tended to be limited to living standards, wide education, administrative efficiency, and new types of personal freedom. It rarely went far toward approving ultimate values and life goals.

THE UNIVERSITY EXPERIENCE

The objective of the Mexican university student was educational and his major adjustments to the United States took place in association with the university community. Here we will examine some of the adjustment problems of the student with respect to the university itself and the extent to which he succeeded in his academic goals.

We have already mentioned the language difficulty in connection with social adjustment. It obviously was also a source of major academic difficulty. Nevertheless, language inadequacy by itself did not prevent satisfactory academic adjustment and achievement. Only when coupled with personal maladjustments, inadequate academic preparation, or lack of motivation did the language handicap lead to academic failure.

Many faculty members and persons concerned with educational exchange have urged stricter selection of foreign students on the basis of language ability. It is true that the linguistic handicap causes foreign students to be more trouble to the university and to the professors than native students. But in itself it is not diagnostic of the future success or failure of the student. One of the most able graduate students of our core group would have been barred from his academic career had strict language requirements been enforced. Despite the difficulties and personal frustrations arising from his early inadequacy, the world of scholarship would have been the loser had he not been admitted to the university.

Baldovinos and Pérez Castro in their study of Mexican holders of fellowships in the agricultural sciences point out that 90 per cent of the fellowship holders came here with an inadequate command of spoken English.[4] However, during the first semester in the United States, students judged to have a good command of spoken English made no better grades than students with inadequate command and 10 per cent of those with good English made poor academic records and were unsuccessful on their return to Mexico. (The numbers involved probably are too small to make this statement significant.) They cite the case of a student who was rejected by one fellowship program because of his poor English but accepted by another on the basis of his academic preparation, ability, and motivation. He subsequently achieved the master of science and doctor of science degrees at a United States university in two years and nine months.

No doubt special classes in English for foreigners such as are offered at UCLA and in many other institutions are of considerable help in overcoming the initial handicap. However, such courses are of little aid to the

[4] G. Baldovinos and C. Pérez Castro, *Programa de Becas para Estudiantes Mexicanas de Ciéncias Agrícolas* (Mexico City: Investigaciones Industriales, Banco de México, S.A., 1951), pp. 49–50.

student with his other academic work in his first semester. At UCLA students required to take the course in English for foreigners are limited in the number of other courses they are allowed to take. Baldovinos and Pérez Castro suggest that a one to two months' intensive English training course, such as the summer course offered at the University of Michigan, is far more effective than concurrent courses. During a short, intensive course the student is neither distracted by the problems of other academic courses, nor involved in the first major adjustments to American university life.

In the core interview group at UCLA, three students on fellowships had a better command of English than privately financed students. In terms of grades, however, one of these essentially failed his first year and another made only mediocre grades, although both seemed well prepared. One privately financed student with little English difficulty was asked to withdraw because of inadequate preparation.

Evidence on orientation courses as aids to student adjustment is inadequate. Only two of the students interviewed had passed through an orientation course (at the University of Texas). They were grateful for the attention they received and spoke highly of the facilities, staff, course content, and intention, but voiced two criticisms. Both felt that they had been inadequately briefed on the grading system and the structure of the American university. They also felt that in a sense they were treated too well, resulting in a temporary sense of disillusionment when they reached UCLA. At the University of Texas, housing facilities were provided, there were many organized social events, and they were made to feel important through opportunities to meet prominent people. After their arrival at UCLA, despite the well-organized services of the Foreign Student Adviser's Office, they were "on their own." The available housing that they could afford was inferior, there was much less social life, and they no longer met "important people." Both recognized this as inevitable and suggested that the orientation program should more approximate university conditions. It is our impression that good orientation programs facilitate student adjustments. On the other hand, the better informed and better prepared the student is, the less benefit he will get from the orientation program. On this basis, benefits to Mexican students will be less than to students from other countries.

A second cluster of university adjustment problems related to the students' lack of preparation for the competitive grading system, as mentioned above; administrators' difficulties in evaluating courses and degrees from Mexican institutions; and inadequate academic counseling. When they were counseled, our Mexican students tended to take the adviser's suggestions as final and often were not aware that there were electives or options in meeting requirements. As a result they sometimes did not take the courses of most interest and value to them. On the other hand, undergraduate students were often resentful of requirements outside their field of specialization. This attitude is not unknown among American students.

Mention already has been made of the difficulties of finding housing and establishing social relationships. In a large metropolitan university, these probably are not problems peculiar to the foreign student. If foreign students were made aware of this fact, their adjustment would probably be easier.

An adequately staffed and properly oriented Foreign Student Adviser's Office evidently is of considerable aid in adjustment, both to the United States and to the university. Mexican students at UCLA spoke well of the office there. They apparently did not regard it as part of the formal university administration and their comments suggest that this separation is desirable if the office is to be effective. Formal efforts through organized group activities to provide some social adjustment were not regarded by Mexican students as very successful. It is doubtful if the office could aid in establishing the more intimate personal relations with American students which the Mexican student seems to desire. Neither can it always deal effectively with complicated academic problems.

Insofar as the goal of student exchange is academic achievement, the Mexican students in our sample clearly overcame the difficulties of adjustment to the university. Mexican students, at least at the University of California, evidently were a highly selected and well-prepared group. Contrary to most faculty impressions, undergraduate Mexican students were more successful in their first year than were foreign students from a number of other countries. They also were more successful than either incoming freshmen from American high schools or American students entering the university with advanced standing.

An analysis of the undergraduate grade records of foreign students and of American transfer students for a six-year period on the Berkeley and Los Angeles campuses of the University of California was made in 1952 by the Board of Admissions and Relations with Schools (see Table 5). Examination of records of transfer students both at Berkeley and Los

Table 5. Median Grade-Point Averages of Selected Undergraduate Students during Their First Semester at the University of California *

Status on Admission	Berkeley		Los Angeles	
	Number of Students	GPA†	Number of Students	GPA†
Freshmen				
California high school graduates meeting standard entrance requirements..........	6,055	1.39	6,009	1.31
Out-of-state high school graduates meeting standard entrance requirements..........	277	1.39	400	1.33
Transfers with advanced standing				
From California junior colleges				
Eligible from high school..........	1,456	1.43	1,889	1.38
Ineligible from high school..........	2,103	1.07	3,871	1.07
From Los Angeles..........	1,255	1.54	...	1.41
From Berkeley..........	...	...	583	1.51
From California private colleges..........	695	1.44	667	1.51
Out-of-state under regular rules..........	578	1.47	1,636	1.35
Out-of-state with 60 units complete..........	899	1.48	201	1.34
Foreign students both freshmen and with advanced standing				
Austria	9	1.74	9	1.93
Canada	91	1.49	58	1.34
China	132	1.58	32	1.27
England	34	1.61	41	1.17
France	17	1.59	21	1.63
Germany	52	1.87	25	1.43
India	71	1.06	15	0.73
Japan	29	1.66	51	1.51
Latin America (six countries excluding Mexico)..........	77	1.20	44	1.02
Mexico	14	1.70	15	1.39
Norway	34	1.20	11	1.10
Sweden	11	1.61	3	1.28
All foreign students, 1946–52..........	1,121	1.46	...	...

Source: Report, Board of Admissions and Relations with Schools, University of California, December 1952, mimeographed.
* Varying dates are covered, but most figures are for 1946–52.
† Highest possible GPA (grade point average) is 3. A letter grade of "A" equals 3 grade points, "B" equals 2, "C" equals 1, "D," "E," and "F" equal 0. Graduation requires grade-point average of 1 or more, depending upon the college.

Angeles suggests that undergraduate standards are relatively high at both places. Comparable figures for graduate students are not available.

The numbers of foreign students from particular countries are often too small to allow generalizations with statistical reliability, but general trends probably are significant. At Berkeley, undergraduate foreign students as a group made higher grade-point averages than did any categories of entering freshmen, and their averages approximate the averages of the highest categories of students entering with advanced standing, except for transfers from the Los Angeles campus. Comparable figures are not available for the Los Angeles campus.

Comparison of Mexican undergraduates with other selected groups shows that in their first semester they made higher grade-point averages than did entering freshmen of any category in Table 5 and compared favorably with students entering with advanced standing from United States institutions. At Berkeley, where records of Mexican students entering as freshmen are segregated, Mexican students entering with advanced standing were significantly above the average of United States students entering with advanced standing. In general, Mexican undergraduates made better records than did students from most other Latin American countries. They also made better records on the average than did students from Canada, China, England, India, Norway, and Sweden. At Los Angeles they did somewhat less well than students from Austria, Germany, France, Japan, Portugal, and Spain. At Berkeley, however, the relative situation was reversed for most of these groups: Mexican students made higher averages than all the groups named except Austrian and German students.

If the relative level of accomplishment of Mexican students holds for other institutions, problems of crucial importance are raised. Differences from other Latin American students may reflect higher standards in Mexican education, although improvements in Mexican schools over the past thirty years have been primarily in the direction of broadening the availability of education rather than in the direction of raising its quality. Moreover, such an explanation on the basis of higher standards seems inadequate in view of the variable performance of students from different European countries. It may well be, therefore, that the significant variables lie more in the nature of selection processes and motivations (possibly more Mexican students were self-selected and self- or family-financed) and in some cases perhaps in the degree to which the total society has moved in the direction of western European and United States models. For some countries the relative quality and accessibility of university training may determine whether the best students go abroad or study at home. In the present state of our knowledge a choice between these possible factors (if indeed a single factor can explain the situation) seems quite hazardous.

At the graduate level the picture is less clear. However, of seven students who enrolled in the Graduate Division at Los Angeles and who formed part of the core group, one withdrew because of emotional disturbances, one withdrew because he was advised that he would probably fail, one was persuaded to become a candidate for an M.A. degree, instead of the doctorate which he had originally aspired to, one was here for one year and not a candidate for a higher degree but apparently made satisfactory grades. Another, at UCLA for only one year, made unsatisfactory grades, but felt he had received the technical training he wanted. Two seemed likely to complete the doctorate if they continued, and a seventh, actually engaged in post-doctoral medical study, had both received a job offer in the United States and been awarded a Guggenheim fellowship. It is our impression that a random selection of seven United States students entering the UCLA graduate school might show no better pattern of success.

Objectively, then, Mexican students as a whole appeared to succeed academically. Such an objective evaluation, however, may not coincide with the students' subjective evaluations of their own achievements. These will be considered later.

SUMMARY

Although, for reasons already indicated, it is impossible to define precise adjustment stages for Mexican students, we believe all members of the core group who succeeded in completing the year of study — eight out of ten — had "come to terms" with the United States. This does not mean that they had solved all adjustment problems. Several had continuing economic difficulties that created frustrations and tensions, but these problems are not really the results of their United States experience. Of the four members of the core group who originally came for one year, two would have liked to stay a second year, one succeeded in doing so, and the fourth has a reasonable expectation of returning. On the other hand, none of the core group, regardless of length of stay, had been "seduced" by United States culture; all expected to return ultimately to Mexico although they hoped to be able to do so on their own terms. Primary loyalties and orientations toward Mexico persisted even among students who had formed close personal ties.

Although data are not so full for the noninterview group, they point in the same direction. Except for one student who appeared to reject both United States and Mexican culture, only one had been "seduced" and intends to remain. (One other person who might be so classed actually was brought here by relatives with the intention of remaining.)

In contrast with many foreign student groups, for example the Indians and Japanese,[5] the Mexican student arrived with greater knowledge of objective aspects of United States life and with more prior contact with Americans. Although probably all Mexicans are at least latently anti-American, the majority of the students had qualified their sentiments before arrival. Even those retaining some active hostility recognized the superiority of the United States in some technical fields and had come to this country to improve their knowledge and skills.

Thus in many respects the adjustment of most Mexican students was relatively easy. However much the student might decry our materialism, he enjoyed the greater comfort, ease, and orderliness of United States life. Students of middle- or upper-class status generally felt that they were accepted in the United States, at least on a superficial level, however much they might regret their inability to form closer associations with Americans than had been possible. Language difficulties were bothersome in social and academic adjustment but most failures in adjustment clearly seemed due either to deep-seated prior personality problems or to inadequate ability or academic preparation. Some evidence exists that Mexican students on the average were at least as successful academically as American students.

[5] See Lambert and Bressler, *op. cit.*; the Bennett *et al.* study of Japanese students is in manuscript.

4

Opinions and Reactions

IN THE previous chapter we described some of the ways in which the Mexican student adapts to life in the United States. In this chapter we propose to examine in more detail the ways in which the Mexican student reacts to these experiences and to explore the opinions and attitudes he holds or develops. The focus here will be upon the student after he has achieved some measure of adjustment. Where pertinent, we will discuss the degree to which preconceptions have altered, where knowledge has increased, shifts of opinions and attitudes, affective relationships, and satisfactions and dissatisfactions. These problems will be discussed in relation to the American university, to selected aspects of American life, and to the United States and its relations to the rest of the world.[1]

THE UNIVERSITY

The general reactions of Mexican students suggest that they find the American university experience satisfying and approve of the American university professor. To a specific question in the Sentence Completion Test (see the Appendix) the students, with few exceptions, answered either that the professor respected the student or that the student approved of the professor. Such responses came even from students with very antagonistic attitudes toward much of their American experience. Most dissatisfactions with the university center around inadequacies in social relationships and administrative procedures rather than around the university as an intellectual experience. Two background considerations have

[1] In somewhat different form, parts of this chapter have been presented in Ralph L. Beals, "The Mexican Student Views the United States," *Annals of the American Academy of Political and Social Science*, 295:108–15 (September 1954).

relevance here: the prestige and influence of the intellectual in Mexican society, and the fact that most students are drawn from the classes for which education is a positive value.

A common student criticism is of the grading system of the American university with its frequent examinations, the resulting preoccupation with grades on the part of the American student, and the highly competitive attitudes of the students. These patterns are more characteristic of Mexican secondary schools than of Mexican universities. Even students who pass through orientation centers apparently are not adequately prepared for this aspect of the American university, and two students insisted that the university grading system was never mentioned in their orientation course. But if general reactions appear favorable, the interview materials suggest specific areas and situations of gratification and dissatisfaction. Thus Isabella Lopez expressed surprise at the possibilities open to the American student: "I always had the feeling that Europeans or even Latin Americans had a more complete education; that is, a wider scope. But you have lots of subjects they don't give there. Only they are not compulsory." On the other hand, as a result of competition, students tend to specialize in a very few subjects and few get the breadth of training which is available to them. She remarked, "It shocks me sometimes the things students can do in order to lower a curve or make a grade." While she had always found students helpful in lending notes or in other ways, she heard of cases where students had refused to lend notes. "And that's something you don't think of in Latin America." In Mexico, she often had had oral examinations which gave, she felt, a closer contact with the professor than was possible with large groups and frequent written examinations.

After further experience with the grading system she remarked: "I think it's good in one way because it's statistical (based on 'how the group is behaving'). But you don't get a personal, individual idea of how they are doing. And I think I told you I don't like impersonal teaching." These comments all applied, of course, to undergraduate instruction.

Initially, she felt quite lost in the university. She had difficulty obtaining entrance to the graduate school. Her degree of *pasante* was rejected and her Mexican school interpreted as not of university grade because the word "Polytechnic" appeared in its name. Isabella then went to the chairman of her department, told him about the courses she had taken, and the chairman wrote a letter which resulted in her acceptance as a graduate student. However, she was unclassified for one semester on the grounds that her grades were low.

She later expanded about her experience on arrival. "I thought I would be accepted as a student here. I was very disappointed when I wasn't. And, I must be frank about it, I always thought I had a higher level of background than most foreign students." Of the graduate office she said: "They didn't know anything of the system in our country. And I thought that if the graduate division had lots of foreign students coming in and out, they should at least have a pattern or a list or something of the differences between the countries where they received more students — and they didn't have the slightest idea of the system in Mexico. And that was the reason why I wasn't accepted." After several experiences with the office, she remarked: "I still think that they don't know anything about procedures in other countries. I think it's all right to have strict rules — it's all right to have strict rules for the United States and the state of California, because I have heard that the people who come from other universities have the same trouble I had. The university can get well-organized in other respects, so I couldn't see why they couldn't get well-organized in that respect." She was unable to see either the dean or any of the assistant deans and spoke only to clerical attendants in the office. Her impression of these was "bad, immediately. Because they say, 'Well, this is the rule and that's that.' I was almost on the verge of screaming at them, and not enrolling because I thought it was final."

Asked whether she thought the attitudes expressed by people in the office of the graduate division were characteristic of the whole university, she replied: "I don't think so. I think it's characteristic of bureaucrats all over the world, because you get exactly the same feeling in Mexico — rules — here they are very polite usually, and they stick to the rules, but in Mexico it's just horrible. But I imagine it's the characteristic of bureaucrats." She felt that bureaucratic attitudes were more common in administration offices than in department offices. In the latter she found clerical people and secretaries very helpful. Regarding the Foreign Student Adviser's Office, she remarked: "I think they are quite nice. It is quite different, entirely different from the graduate division. And that's the same feeling that I have had in my own department and in my husband's department — they try to help you. I like it because you are a new student — a foreign student and a new student both."

Isabella commented on the fact that the mixing of students of different levels meant that courses she expected to be specialized were actually quite general. She saw considerable differences between undergraduate and graduate work. She felt that American students as a group (it should be noted here that Isabella was a teaching assistant) have no personality in the sense of any organized and conscious direction.

During her first semester she had difficulties with some courses but found others easy. She was confused and annoyed to discover that the content of courses often was quite different from what the title led her to expect. But she remarked of the American professor: "It's very impressive to see how up-to-date he is in his field." She found professors often willing to arrange special examinations to take into account her language difficulties and difference in training. "I have found that the professors are extremely helpful. It's because I am a foreign student that they are extra nice; but everybody has been very helpful in the department."

She had expected that relations with professors would be more informal, in contrast to Europe or Latin America, and she found them so. About this she remarked: "You still respect them, but they don't mind if you don't 'take off your hat' every time you see them, and you can more or less talk your problems over with them, personal problems, and they are more easy to approach than they are in Mexico." She pointed out that at times discipline in class is difficult because of the informality and when she became a teaching assistant she felt she had to insist on not being called by her first name. Despite her shyness, she became a very successful teaching assistant and an effective disciplinarian. She felt that her social contacts with the faculty were greater in the United States than would be possible in Mexico, but she had difficulty making friends. She found people in her husband's department (a social science) rather distressing because the students always talked shop; in her own department (a biological science) people talked about many other subjects.

She felt that neither Los Angeles nor the university is cosmopolitan in the sense that Mexico City and San Francisco are. She attributed this to the dispersed character of the city and the absence of college life at UCLA. "After five you don't see anyone and you don't get to know anyone either. The only social contact you have is with foreign students in the international house and with Americans, well, the people we know in the department, but I don't think we know a lot of other people from other departments." She found transportation a problem because it prevented her from having much social life or attending exhibits, concerts, and other cultural events.

When Maria Chávez came to UCLA she found no dormitories, and was forced to take an apartment with another girl. She felt strange about this because in Mexico the interpretation placed upon two girls' living in an apartment would be unfavorable. She was confused by registering and filling out papers she did not quite understand, and had to ask many questions.

She found it easiest to make friends with foreign students and felt this was valuable but wished that she might have had more relations with American students. Her courses were hard and she had trouble with the technical language. Her first semester she made an A, a B, and two C's. One of the C's, in a theory course, she considered her own responsibility. The course was presented well and had value. The other C she blamed upon the professor. She believed that most students got a C in the course, and commented further that the professor talked so rapidly and the terminology was so confusing that she could hardly take notes. However, she said American students had had the same experience. Similarly, she found the professors easier to talk to in the courses in which she made good grades than in those in which she did poorly. Examinations at first made her unduly nervous but in her second semester she felt much more confident.

She was disappointed in her first semester because she was prevented from taking some courses she wished to take. Generally she felt her university experience was valuable although she did not learn as much as she had expected to. She found particularly useful her observation of the very different methods of teaching in the United States. In retrospect, she felt that she might have studied more, but on the other hand that much of the value of her experience had been gained outside of the classroom.

Roberto Rosales likewise said that he had associated mainly with foreign students. He was not entirely happy about this and on one occasion he lived with an Indian group, which he didn't like at all. "Perhaps we had the same opinion of each other . . . we had troubles always with the kitchen and dishes and they were very dirty and I hated that." He felt that his experience with Americans was most important to him, but, although he belonged to an international student club, he thought that American students didn't attend very often. His most valued experiences were with older Americans, but he did not elaborate on their character.

78

Roberto's grades in the university were quite poor. He attributed this partly to language difficulty. He claimed he understood his courses but was unable to write adequate examinations. Indirectly he confessed to insufficient study for in his second semester he said he was studying harder. Roberto virtually failed in his one year at UCLA, but grades meant little to him. He expressed disappointment only at not improving his English more. Otherwise, he insisted that he gained a great deal from his year here. Courses in his field in Mexico are "too theoretical," he said, whereas in the United States they have much more practical application. Because he is interested in application, his feeling of satisfaction may be justified. Had he been able to spend more time in the United States, he perhaps would have preferred an apprenticeship in an American business. One of his hopes for the future was to get a job with an American company in Mexico that would send him back to the United States for apprenticeship-type training. Roberto apparently had no contacts with American professors outside of class. He felt special consideration should be given to difficulties the foreign student may face but he thought that regardless of their origin students should be expected to know the materials in their courses and were entitled to no preference in grades.

Gonzalo Reyes observed that American students may discuss politics but without the passion there is in Mexico. He felt that students here are more interested in football and in parties. "I think the intellectual group is very small here. Here in the library they didn't talk very much about anything else but making an A or B or passing the course . . . they go to the library but they don't discuss American poets or European poets . . . I feel the Mexican student grows up much faster than here." He also pointed out that the American professor gives all his time to the university whereas the Mexican professor gains his livelihood in occupations outside the school, often unrelated to the subject he teaches. Being a professor in Mexico hence is usually a matter of prestige. The professor gives his lectures but is not concerned with taking roll. Examinations are oral and allow the student an opportunity for contact and discussion with the professor and the professor may take a more personal interest in the individual as a result. If the student fails an examination, there is no probation or other discipline; he simply repeats the examination. "The student is more interested in educating himself. Here I think the universities treat you like high school. They tell you you have to go to class. You have so many attendances. You have to do your homework."

Alberto Vásquez thought he learned most in courses where he liked the professor. He considered that his major initial difficulty was with language. In a special English course for foreign students he made a grade of C. He came to the United States with high hopes of studying either bacteriology or chemistry. He went to the University of Chicago and was put in the college program, and was unable to follow the studies he wished. As a result, he thought that one of the biggest mistakes in his career was going to Chicago, but had found what he wished by transferring to UCLA.

Before Alberto came to the United States he thought that an American university was something very specialized. He did not think in terms of a university like UCLA but of just two or three buildings where one stayed all the time working in laboratories. Despite this difference from his expectations, he liked UCLA very much. He did not realize at first that he could have freedom in taking courses; consequently he did not try to think about his own program but took what his advisers told him to take. He expected professors to be very formal but found them informal — so informal, in fact, that he thought the professor did not inspire respect in the students. But after he became accustomed to the informality, he considered it natural. "The American professor likes to joke in class and likes to make his point with some humor; while the Mexican professor likes to make his point with his own authority and tries to be very serious. The relations between the student and the instructors are very different. I feel free to ask questions in class here, or if I disagree about something I will speak up. In Mexico I would just keep my mouth shut." Despite this he thought that the Mexican professor makes a "better exposition of the subject. He is a little more organized in his lectures. And the American instructor makes his point better because he gets closer to the students, although he isn't organized at all." "Objective" examinations were completely new to Alberto and he found them very confusing, especially since he was at first very slow at reading. He found less association among students than he expected. Before coming he thought the only ways of getting prestige as a student were either to make good grades or to be a famous athlete. Prestige through organized student activities was new to him. He expected no difference in treatment from other students, but he was treated better because of his language difficulties. After he learned to express himself he was treated like any other student.

Rita García claimed that the university was as she expected. She felt the attitudes of American students to be both practical and theoretical. If she asked them a question, they seemed to need not only to give her an answer, but to tell her the meaning of it. She felt this required a lot of education and she liked it. Asked if she had a preference among universities in the United States, she said she would return to UCLA because she has formed an attachment for the place, "the students, the buildings and the trees, everything — you know when you are in a place and do things there you like it, it's part of you, you feel it."

Asked about a professor of Spanish origin she said he was "very nice, very good person, very helpful, very Americanized . . . he's practical, very fine person, doesn't waste any time in talking like the Spanish American people."

Rita felt that students at the University were not so friendly as students in Mexico. Her best friends were foreign students. She felt though that perhaps this was because they were more mature and more understanding. She "likes Americans but . . ."

Enrique Jiménez was working essentially on post-doctoral training. He was to some extent accepted as an equal by the faculty and his reactions hence were somewhat different from other students'. He had many social invitations from faculty members, but practically no interaction with other foreign students. All the people he met at UCLA he thought were very nice and he liked them all very much. He came intending to work for another degree but on arrival discovered that in his field this would be relatively meaningless. He believed he was accomplishing his ends and both his objective record and the offers of jobs and fellowships he received indicated that this was true. He felt that he had been very well treated at UCLA and that he was received simply, openly, and very warmly by his department chairman, whom he knew to be a scientist of international distinction. Much of his work was in laboratories and he expressed great admiration for the "organization" of the university: when experimental materials were needed in the laboratory he was able to get them quickly and easily. (By 1956 his research was widely known for its importance and originality.)

Juan Ortega was a married graduate student who had spent several years at a midwestern university. In general he objected to the competitiveness among American students, which he attributed in part to the grading system and which, he felt, focuses attention on getting grades rather than getting an education. He commented that premedical students are hated by students in some departments because of their competitive-

81

ness. He saw a certain rigidity about requirements in the university. (Actually most Mexican university curriculums are much narrower and much more rigid. Perhaps the difference is that the requirements here force a spread of interests at the undergraduate level, where the Mexican system forces a concentration.) He thought that the student who wants to get a good education can do so at an American university, but that those who are not really interested in getting an education may receive a rather inferior one.

He was in a rather large department and sensed a definite social stratification among the graduate students, with an inner clique which it was hard for the new student to enter. In contrast with his experiences in a midwestern university, he found that friendships were more difficult to make at UCLA and that contacts with the faculty were on a more formal basis. He thought large classes were partly responsible for the undergraduate grading system. He was shocked by the attitude of some graduate students who looked upon their graduate training as a business proposition rather than a furthering of genuine intellectual interests. He was distressed that his work load (he was a teaching assistant) and his study load prevented him from doing more reading, including reading outside his field. He missed many cultural and recreational opportunities because he could not afford a car. He mentioned particularly missing concerts, but actually he did not attend the concerts given on campus.

He thought that at the classroom level the university had no policy toward foreign students. Hence the individual instructor set his own policy. Some instructors made an effort to help the foreign student or make allowances for him; others did not.

Of his own department, he spoke of the faculty as being on one side of the fence and the graduate students on the other side. He thought this undesirable. At his midwestern university, two faculty members were very good friends of his. In contrast he remarked that, at UCLA, "you don't see the head of the department going down to the graduate students' office and saying 'What about a cup of coffee at the commons?'" Despite the existence of this "fence," he said he would have no hesitation about going to a member of the faculty to discuss an idea or a problem. But he felt that the faculty members considered this consultation part of their job and had no personal interest in him. (Actually several faculty members had considerable personal interest in Juan but apparently were unable to communicate this.) He thought that few American professors are really excited about the subjects they teach. He attributed this partly to an emphasis on research, "the sort of competition that you get in academic professions here — publish, publish, publish!"

He felt driven hard by his work. "We are meeting our friends less and less so we don't have any chance for discussions which I like very much." His recreation consisted mainly of getting together with people from the department for beer parties, going to the movies or occasionally to a concert, and on rare occasions going out to dinner.

Arturo Ortiz when interviewed was in his second period at UCLA. Earlier he had been there as an undergraduate and at the time of interviewing was a graduate student. Arturo originally came to UCLA on a wartime training program and had no idea of the expenses involved. When he decided he would like to continue, he talked with his professors and asked how much money further study would require. In retrospect, he realized that they pretended ignorance because they knew he could not raise the money; instead they secured another fellowship for him. Even so, he had to seek part-time work in order to continue his studies.

On his first visit he was accommodated in a fraternity house. He reported that none of the Latin American students housed with him were used to such things as making their own beds, sweeping the floor, and washing their own clothes, so most of them moved out to regular boarding houses. He felt his greater maturity helped him to stay the entire time and adapt to the situation. The fraternity members were, he said, very nice to him and invited him to parties. Actually he found the social life difficult because it took so much of the time he needed for study. When he proposed to leave the fraternity to save money for an expensive operation he needed, the fraternity manager arranged for him to work for his board and room. So he learned to wash dishes, wash clothes, and set the table. He remarked, "It was fun — I liked it, because it was the first time." (Significantly, Arturo is not of upper-class origin.) In his first visit to UCLA Arturo felt his teachers were all "just like another God." On his second visit he still felt that he should respect a person who had a doctor's degree but he did not necessarily consider this made him a superior human being. But he thought his teachers did a great deal for him and were always ready to help. Regarding instruction, he considered that in his particular scientific field teaching methods were far in advance of what they were in Mexico. He did not necessarily learn more here than he would have in Mexico, but he learned much faster.

AMERICAN LIFE WAYS

In Chapter 2 we discussed some of the preconceptions of the Mexican student about life in the United States and in Chapter 3 we discussed some of his experiences in residence. Now we will consider what the Mexican student came to think about some aspects of life in this country. The discussion cannot be as precise as we would like, for we have insufficient data to assess the opinions and attitudes of students in relation to the length of time they had been in the country or to their varying backgrounds and interests. Discussion is based on both interviews and written instruments. The data from returned students are very similar.

The aspects of American life selected for consideration all seem to be pertinent to the experience of the majority of Mexican students. Moreover, their reactions to many of these aspects seem to follow fairly consistent patterns. Yet it must constantly be remembered that Mexicans vary individually. Some had much more foreknowledge than others. Those with technical goals frequently came with essentially neutral attitudes toward the United States, others came with either very hostile or relatively favorable images of the United States and these attitudes underwent little change. However, the majority of students who stayed any length of time grew in knowledge and understanding. They abandoned some of their preconceptions and clung to others. Most of them spoke of things and persons they liked and others they disliked in America. Some saw themselves as informed but not unfriendly critics. None wished to make Mexico over into the image of the United States, yet all but the most persistently hostile not only acquired skills and knowledge they believed they could use for the welfare of Mexico but ideas about the social changes desirable in Mexico. Yet even when students felt they had discovered social relationships or attitudes or institutions worth emulating, they favored adaptations to the Mexican scene rather than uncritical transference.

It must be emphasized also that, just as the Mexican student arrived with partial and inconsistent preconceptions about the United States, he left with partial and inconsistent impressions of it. His knowledge might be more complete, but he had not become equally familiar with all aspects of American culture and society, nor did his images and his attitudes form a coherent and consistent whole.

Democracy and Politics. Most students found much to admire in the political life of the United States. The conduct of government, the widespread and effective participation in the political process, the conduct of campaigns and elections, and the orderly transfer of power were all considered evidence of functioning political democracy. However, most students distinguished between democracy in the political process and democracy in social relationships. Criticisms of American democracy usually centered upon such social aspects as the treatment of minority groups. Many students also saw serious threats to the future of American political democracy. These points will be discussed later.

Actually Mexican students knew little in detail about American politics. About state and local affairs and most domestic issues they were relatively uninformed; few could define the differences between the Democratic and Republican parties or identify such nationally known political figures as Taft, Acheson, and Dulles. One indeed at election time in 1952 thought Stevenson was the Republican candidate! Most were influenced by the charismatic quality of Eisenhower and favored him for the presidency, including a student who thought him a Democrat. Others, although attracted by him, either disapproved of his military background or, while approving of Eisenhower, associated his supporters with the forces of economic imperialism or isolationism.

Despite their ignorance of current political affairs, students commented on the people's greater political activity here. Initiative and referendum procedures in California were singled out particularly, and the fact that even where these were lacking, people feel free to write to their legislators and that these letters receive consideration. Contact with governmental bureaucracy often produced unfavorable reactions, especially disagreeable encounters with the customs and immigration services. One student who had crossed the border several times took pains to recite instances of special courtesy and consideration but clearly these were less important in his thinking than one extremely unpleasant experience. On the other hand, the absence of the system of *mordida* impressed students, although there was some suspicion, supported by citations of cases, that perhaps in the United States bribery is present but only where large sums are involved.

Many students expressed apprehension about the future of American political democracy. One group interpreted what Seymour Lipset[2] has called "The Radical Right" as evidence of a strong trend toward fascism. The radical right was also identified with the forces favoring economic

[2] Seymour Martin Lipset, "The Radical Right: A Problem for American Democracy," *British Journal of Sociology*, 6:176–209 (June 1955).

imperialism in Latin America and this fact colored the whole attitude of many toward United States politics as well as toward our international policies. Students in 1952–53 were generally reluctant to discuss frankly the trends and events they considered fascistic. Usually, they said, they either professed ignorance or agreed with their hosts, for they really feared retaliation if they spoke freely. Several students refused to have their remarks recorded but in both recorded interviews and unrecorded conversations the words "McCarthyism" and "McCarranism" were used repeatedly.

Some also feared the influence of propaganda and the controlled mass media; but some saw resistance to it. As Maria Chávez remarked, "As far as I have been able to realize, the American people are very influenced by propaganda. One example is that in one store they say that navy blue is the color of the month and then all the people are wearing navy blue suits . . . but on the other hand, I think that apart from any propaganda if the people are going to do something, in general they don't care about propaganda; and if they are not in accordance with that propaganda they will go against it and they won't do it."

In their opinions about United States social democracy, many students had contradictory attitudes. Most Mexicans tended to see the United States as a classless or relatively classless society. On the average they were less aware of class differences in the United States than American students are. And those who had experience with economically secure and reasonably educated working people had this view reinforced.

On the other hand students generally were highly critical of some aspects of both political and social democracy in the United States. The need to be critical had two sources. One group included those who were most apprehensive of the fascistic trends they thought they perceived in the United States. Usually these same students were also the most critical of what they termed the economic imperialism of the United States. Other students who were critical apparently felt the need for some defense following their admission that political democracy functioned better in the United States than in Mexico.

Criticism usually took two forms. One was the accusation that the United States was not interested in democracy outside its borders. In support of this accusation, students usually cited cases of what they considered economic imperialism, interference in the struggles for democracy in Latin American countries, and the support of undemocratic Latin

American governments. Students advancing these views usually also presented the second major type of criticism as well.

Much more common than the foregoing was to accuse Americans of hypocrisy because we do not apply the democratic creed we follow in politics in our social relationships, particularly in our discrimination against Negroes. Probably no other aspect of United States life was viewed so unfavorably or mentioned so often. But, as mentioned elsewhere, discrimination against Mexican-Americans commonly was viewed as having a class basis or as being similar to discrimination in Mexico. A student deeply moved by the treatment of the Negro could say: "Of course, we know that Mexicans are discriminated against in a social way, because they are poor; but if they are rich they are not discriminated [against]. I think people in Mexico believe that Mexican-Americans are discriminated [against] not exactly because they are Mexican but because they are poor and ignorant, just as they would be discriminated [against] in Mexico."

Mention of discrimination against other ethnic groups occurred only if the individual had observed it. Only a few students who had spent some time in the United States and who were interested in politics and democracy developed an awareness of the historical background of Negro discrimination and the extent of recent changes. A frequent distinction was made between Texas and the rest of the United States: "Texas is the black sheep." It may be added that none of the students interviewed knew much about the rest of the South. In the main, Mexicans were uninformed about the political and social history of the United States.

Economic Life. Students expected to find a high standard of living. The United States is "a big country with civilized people, all of them, or at least most of them, having a high standard for living well . . . I knew that . . . the worker of a factory has his own car and his refrigerator . . . all the things that make for a comfortable living which in Mexico our laborers don't have." In general these preconceptions were borne out. Students recognized that there were poor people in the United States but those with more extensive contacts found the material level of living and the extent of education even greater than they had expected.

One major change in opinions was lessened hostility toward "big business" and a recognition that competition in business is still possible despite the concentration of economic power. Possibly because so many of them were drawn from families that are working toward the industrialization of Mexico, Mexican students on the average were more favorable

87

toward concentrations of power in business (and government) than were American students asked the same questions. Despite the existence of a group with a "businessman's philosophy," there was general acceptance of such things in Mexico as nationalization of petroleum and the entry of the government into other fields of basic economic development. In part this probably stemmed from their recognition of the impossibility of developing sufficiently large concentrations of private capital in Mexico for many expensive undertakings, coupled with rejection of too-extensive reliance upon foreign capital.

Several students believed that the United States economic system is integrated and directed toward socially useful ends. "It is a system at the least more practical [than the Mexican]; it is a system that . . . I consider to have the aspect of a great machine in which, although a little piece alone is nothing, together all the parts work toward a common end with the result that all work to give a firm base to the country."

On the other hand, some students were relatively indifferent to the United States economic system. Those ideologically associated with the agrarian-nationalist phase of the revolution were more apt to reject it and to favor cooperative and governmental activities in the economic field.

Spiritual versus Materialistic Values. The Mexican student found it possible to accept the technical and economic superiority of the United States because he was buttressed with a sense of the superior spiritual values of his own culture. His opinions on many subjects sometimes changed markedly while he was in the United States, but in most cases he retained his sense of the moral superiority of Mexican life.

The main changes occurred as a result of the discovery of greater social consciousness on the part of Americans than the students had expected, and the realization that family life and morals were better, that there was more interest in literature, music, and the arts, and that Americans were more religious than they anticipated. Changes in attitudes toward social and family life will be discussed later.

Many Mexicans came to recognize that basically the interest in money, good houses, better clothing, and the ownership of cars and various gadgets actually is no greater in the United States than in Mexico. The real difference is that these are not realizable goals for many people in Mexico. At the same time, they believed that here these often are the only goals. "The impression we had was that the United States didn't care very much about art or people who really counted. I believed

Americans did not teach anything about living; being phlegmatic, practical, not sentimental, not having poetry . . . Of course, afterwards this changed when I began reading things."

Such changes in attitude were common. Students came to see people in the United States as less superficial and less materialistic, although they still believed in the relative superiority of Mexico in this regard.

Most especially they found Americans more religious than they had expected. The number of Catholics and Catholic churches and the number of Catholics in high places surprised those who had thought of the United States not only as a Protestant country, but as basically irreligious. The common idea of Protestantism as a "church" was dispelled, and sectarian differences often were seen as involving moral issues rather than matters of faith. Several pointed out that Catholicism in the United States is very different from what it is in Mexico and commented on the much higher moral standards of the clergy in the United States and the much smaller tendency for the Catholic Church to interfere in secular affairs. It was a general opinion that Americans, especially the men, attend church much more than do Mexicans.

Discovery that the dichotomy between spiritual and materialistic goals is less sharp than they had anticipated posed a serious threat to the self-esteem of most Mexican students. Only students with an objective sense of cultural relativity seemed undisturbed. A few seemed ripe for alienation, but the great majority took refuge in an iteration of Mexico's moral superiority.

Thus one student admired the high standard of living in the United States but found social patterns "much looser than ours," and thought that the achievement of the high living standard "led them [Americans] to lose all those moral values of our time . . . I still think that almost all the people in the United States think that the only goal in life is to get money, to get work . . . Besides making money, we have another goal."

Socio-Sexual Relationships. Mexican students generally found Americans more courteous to strangers than Mexicans are, although all could cite exceptions. This was true even of women students, who initially were repelled by the lack of formality in the behavior of American men. In addition, as has been recorded about other foreign student groups, they were impressed by the great friendliness of Americans. At the same time, they complained that this was superficial, that Americans are hard to get to know, and that we have little concept of friendship. Although this comment occurs frequently among foreign students, with Mexicans it is a little paradoxical, for all the data indicate that the great majority of Mexicans are either neutral or hostile toward friends (see p. 42).

Some first-year students, as we have indicated, were driven to associate with other foreign (but not Mexican) students because they could not establish enough satisfactory relationships with American students. Such students found the international student clubs helpful but were not enthusiastic about them. But most had been to a number of parties with American students as a result of contacts established in the organized programs. Students here a longer time often seemed to have established as much social contact with Americans as they wished.

The students thought that many of the Americans they came to know accepted them as people. Some, however, felt that they were rejected by some Americans because they were foreign and that other Americans were interested in them solely out of curiosity.

Men especially continued to find the pattern of relationships between the sexes confusing even after several years in the United States. Men and women who most admired the more equalitarian patterns of sex relationships thought many American girls abused their freedom and that they were less concerned to preserve their virginity than Mexican girls. The idea of male virginity, however, was considered too ridiculous for discussion. But male students who had attended some discussions of sex and sex experiences in fraternity houses or other male gatherings considered our disapproval of Latin double standards to be pure hypocrisy.

Despite many reservations, based mainly on disapproval of extreme cases, only a few very traditional Mexican males failed to approve of the greater freedom and equality of women in the United States. Among women students this approval was enthusiastic and on this score alone most if not all women students face difficulties on their return. While marriage and children were the goals of almost all our women students, they wished also to have interests outside the home and planned to work or to pursue a career of some sort after marriage. Unless they marry unusually tolerant Mexican males, they will encounter disillusionment and in any case will meet some family and social disapproval. Although Mexican values are changing in the direction of greater freedom for women, the upper middle class tends toward conservatism in this regard.

Family Relationships. Most students experienced major changes in attitudes toward American family life. Most had believed that the family had virtually vanished from the United States, that divorce was universal, and that children were brought up without any restraints. The majority of students rather quickly perceived that, while their preconceptions were to some extent borne out by reality, family life among the majority of Americans did not conform to their preconceptions. A selective attitude soon developed.

Probably all Mexican students continued to think that there was too much divorce in the United States and the majority continued to disapprove of all divorce. But they soon realized that divorce is not universal. Most, if not all, students still felt that American family life has lost many important functions and qualities, and even those who approved of the greater freedom of women believed that a great many American women abuse this freedom and that men often were too indifferent to their wives and their behavior. Nevertheless, these students also saw virtues in the best examples of American family life. The majority of Mexican students came strongly to favor the less authoritarian structure of the American family, particularly as it relates to child rearing. While they were not so approving as American university students, perhaps the greatest change of attitudes among Mexican students occurred in the field of child-rearing practices. Again the change in attitudes coincides with trends in Mexican culture.

The Meaning of Labor. In few ways does the United States differ from Latin America (and perhaps many other parts of the world) more than in the dignity accorded labor, particularly labor with the hands. The class implications of various types of work in Latin America have been pointed out elsewhere.[3] With few exceptions, Mexican students commented on this difference. Real changes came about in the behavior of many; some men did their own cooking and upper-middle-class girls sometimes took menial jobs.

One student remarked of the United States: "A boy in the middle class or in the upper class or in the high class doesn't mind working in a gas station in order to get money, or working in a grocery store, or selling papers or doing anything. And if a boy of our high class goes and sells papers, or goes to work in a grocery store, well, all the people will talk about him and it's going to be considered a terrible thing for those people who do it . . . 'Can't his family support him?'"

[3] Ralph L. Beals, "Social Stratification in Latin America," *American Journal of Sociology*, 58:237–339 (January 1953).

A girl who worked as a salesclerk for two weeks in a large downtown department store said: "In Mexico, the poor sales ladies go crazy, because there are ten different ladies asking things, and then she brings things to one person, and then she starts with another person, and then she goes back to the first. [Here] I've seen ladies standing there for ten minutes just waiting for you to finish with the sales lady. It was strange for me . . . and the ladies were awfully patient and nice; and there were just two nasty persons, less than I expected, because of my experience in Mexico."

Students were struck not only with the living standards of working people but with their manners. One girl, asked what was her greatest impression from a conducted holiday tour through California, said: "Well, something that impressed me very much was the confidence of the people themselves, because I had a chance to spend the night with families of different classes and some of them were very wealthy families and some of them were from the middle class, and one of them was, I guess, low class. And, for instance, these people in the lower class, had not a fancy house but a very clean house, and the father of this girl was working until 11 or 12 o'clock at night, and he got his hands covered with oil and some paint remover and everything, but he was very clean. His behavior and his way of treating us was exactly the same as the wealthy people, so that they don't feel bad if they are workers and if they have dirty hands, and they try to have the same things that can make life comfortable. In some other countries, in my own country, the people that work with their hands are considered very low, and, well, their behavior is in general really low. So I was surprised that this man was, well, maybe he didn't look as well as the wealthy ones, maybe his manners weren't as good as the other ones, but, in general, it wasn't a great difference."

Individualism and Order. Before arrival many students envisaged the United States as the ultimate expression of mass culture. They expected to find José Ortega y Gasset's picture of the masses justified and exemplified. Students found the mass culture symbolized in various ways. A girl expressed her horror at women's buying identical dresses in stores. A man commented on the blank faces of hurrying downtown crowds. Soon other impressions obtruded and many students came to modify their views. But for most, their ideas remained confused and their images contradictory.

In one form or another virtually every student of both the core group and the group that was not interviewed indicated that what they liked most about the United States was its orderliness. The focus of attention might be on traffic, on the frequency with which people wait their turn, the organization of public offices, the respect for law and order, or the ease of getting laboratory animals. In contrast to Mexico, they felt life is made easier and more satisfying. After a visit home, a strongly anti-American student described an unpleasant incident in Mexico and then exclaimed, "That could never happen in Los Angeles!" Others described fights over politics and automobile accidents and contrasted them with United States procedures.

At the same time students usually discovered a higher level of individuality than they had expected. The greater independence of women and children impressed them particularly. "In Mexico . . . a boy of eighteen years old is really a boy; he belongs completely to his parents. Here an eighteen-year-old boy, he knows how to do things, he knows how to choose between things, he knows how to answer for himself. That's what I mean by individualism."

And another student, who had earlier said, "There exists here a great liberty which is frequently converted into license, a license which is beyond that which is moral," some months later remarked: ". . . here in America they have really a wider freedom than we have back home, in everything. And they have a wider concept of democracy, and their system of education creates more individualistic ways, and they are brought up in a more independent way of thinking . . . The standard of living is more standardized than back home, and that happens with education, *and so the social circle you can live in here is wider than back home.*" (Emphasis supplied.)

Thus what he had previously thought of as a reduction of the individual to the mass came to be seen by this student as the creation of a common basis of understanding which permits wider and freer associations and choices. Such a concept of individualism often is difficult for the Mexican to grasp, for his own ideas of individualism are closely bound up with concepts of *egoismo* and honor (see Chapter 1). But the more perceptive and thoughtful students found that Americans show individuality. And while this was linked still with a selfish individualism and concern with personal goals, they also saw that Americans are concerned with understanding social problems and extending their interest in others beyond the confines of the family. Many were troubled by the inherent contradictions in their images but few attempted to resolve them.

The United States and the World. The Mexican student, as we indicated in Chapter 2, comes to this country with some measure of anti-American feeling. This does not extend to individual Americans he may have known, but except for this, he does not discriminate among various aspects of the United States.

One major shift in the views of most perceptive students was increasingly to discriminate among government, business, and the people. Students also began to make regional distinctions, setting aside Texas and sometimes other portions of the South as centers of overt discrimination and the midwest as a center of isolationism. The student might feel that the government is aggressive but he usually decides that the American people are not imperialistic.

On another dimension, student attitudes toward the position of the United States in the world fell into three categories: the United States in relation to Mexico and Latin America, the United States in relation to the rest of the non-Communist world, and the United States in relation to the Communist world. The reader who expects clear-cut reactions in any of these categories will be disappointed. But the over-all shift was toward better understanding and some increase in favorableness.

The United States and Mexico and Latin America. Most students considered that the government of the United States interferes in the affairs of Latin America and more specifically that at least indirectly it influences Mexican foreign policy. Even more, students considered United States business to be imperialistic in an economic sense. The American people, they thought, are relatively ignorant of Latin America and of Mexico. Although the behavior of some tourists was deplored — taking pictures of unflattering aspects of Mexico, acting as if they owned the country, denigrating Mexico, showing bad manners or bad morals — a surprising number thought that the majority of tourists are well behaved and, though ignorant, really want to learn about Mexico.

Students to whom specific questions were put thought that the United States interferes less in the affairs of Mexico and Latin America than it did twenty or thirty years ago. Most apprehension about the course of United States politics was related to the possible revival of more aggressive attitudes. A number of students deplored American support of fascistic or dictatorial governments in Latin America and elsewhere because the policy is shortsighted. Such governments, they believed, are completely opportunistic and would not hesitate to desert the United States if it was to their advantage. Generally, students believed that the United States

94

does not give enough economic and technical aid to Latin America and that anti–United States sentiment is increasing in Latin America in part for this reason.

Most antagonism centered upon economic imperialism. Students who had been here for some time criticized business and industrial interests rather than the government or the people. Students who had visited banana plantations were emphatic in their opinions, although they conceded that conditions have improved. Oil and mining interests were mentioned frequently as guilty of exploitation.

In the course of their stay, most students modified their antagonism toward foreign capital investments. Under proper safeguards, investments that will strengthen and help develop the national economy were recognized as beneficial. But the practice of paying Mexican and American workers in Mexico on different salary scales obviously created bitter feeling.

The United States in World Affairs. The distinction between the United States' relation to the non-Communist world and its relation to the Communist world, while made by Mexican students, was not clear-cut and the two may best be discussed together. Most students fell into two groups with respect to such programs as the Marshall Plan and the Technical Assistance Programs. One group believed these programs were founded on real altruism and before their arrival had felt that the aid programs were an expression not only of generosity but of real international understanding. Such students were grieved and disappointed to discover how many Americans were indifferent or hostile to these aid programs. Other students thought all foreign aid programs are motivated purely by self-interest. Still others believed foreign aid was motivated solely by the need to keep export markets active. Others saw foreign aid as a method of entrenching American economic control of foreign countries.

The latter group generally thought that both Russia and the United States are expanding their control over other countries. Those interviewed preferred that the United States be in control, for they believed that in contradistinction to Russia, the United States does not attempt to impose an ideology. They believed it easier in the long run for a country to emancipate itself from economic domination than to free itself from ideological domination. Hence the United States is the lesser of the two evils.

With few exceptions the students believed that the United States should maintain a position of strength, both economically and militarily. They believed that the American people want peace and that the United States is not politically or militarily aggressive at the present time. On the other hand, few agreed that the United States is doing everything it can to maintain peace. But none who answered questions on this subject believed that the Russians are doing everything they can to maintain peace either; as one said, "The Russians can be very difficult."

Many feared that the Korean war (then still in progress) might lead to World War III. Nevertheless, they believed that American participation in the Korean war was intended to prevent another world war and that the United States had an inescapable moral obligation to aid the South Koreans. Some of course had no clear opinions.

Probably most Mexican students preferred a neutralist or independent role for Mexico in world affairs. In part they justified this by reference to the many internal problems of the country and its need to spend all its resources in combating poverty. An important component of these attitudes was national pride, a desire to see Mexico as a nation among equals. Yet most realized that open conflict between Russia and the United States would place Mexico in great danger and that Mexico would have no choice but to align itself with the United States. The majority of Mexican students, often with some degree of reluctance, tended to support the United States on the international scene. But it is important to bear in mind that few saw the conflicts between Russia and the United States as a contrast of black and white. The United States was still regarded with suspicion by most and the degree of their support diminished whenever they interpreted actions by this country as a revival of any form of imperialism, support for fascistic or dictatorial governments, support of colonialism, or interference with the internal affairs of other nations. (For some students probably "other democratic nations" should be substituted; many did not see that refusal of recognition of undemocratic governments or withholding technical and financial assistance is also interference in the internal affairs of other nations.) Students further tended to be repelled by propaganda efforts which emphasized the bigness, superiority, wealth, and power of the United States. Favorable attitudes tended to be enhanced by actions which they interpreted as evidence of nonaggressive, peaceful, and non-imperialistic intentions, respect for political and cultural differences, genuine concern with raising the living standards of other countries, and support for democracy (as a generalized value, for few students were very clear as to what they meant by this word).

In summary, some students, particularly those with technical and professional objectives, did not increase their knowledge of the United States or change their attitudes toward it, whether these were initially favorable or unfavorable. Such students by and large accomplished their educational objectives and, on the whole, approved of their educational experience. This seemed true of even the most hostile. It is probable that some students became more hostile toward the United States as a result of their experiences here, but our sample apparently included no such persons. Significantly, perhaps, those who showed the strongest rejection of the United States often also showed the strongest rejection of Mexico.

The majority of the students, as we have indicated, probably came to the United States with less unfavorable attitudes than those of most Mexicans. Insofar as their attitudes altered and their knowledge increased, the changes were selective in nature. With growth of knowledge and understanding, many shifted from being hostile critics to being friendly critics. But they remained critics in some degree. High living standards, orderliness, the greater freedom of social relationships, the less restrictive aspects of American family life (but not extreme cases of freedom), child rearing, freedom for women, open class structure, and the widespread respect for the dignity of labor met with some and often considerable approval. Hostility toward government and business seemed reduced. Racial discrimination usually was even more strongly condemned. The Mexican student remained convinced, almost without exception, of the superiority of Mexican family life (even though he would like to see it less authoritarian and restrictive) and of the superiority of Mexican life goals with their emphasis on spiritual and humanistic values. He further remained or even became a more confirmed Mexican nationalist. But perhaps the most general effect of the sojourn, whether the student was friendly or hostile, was the breaking down of stereotypes. Even if he still considered American culture materialistic or our family life inferior, he learned that not all Americans or American values are materialistic and that the best examples of family life have good qualities.

A full evaluation of the effects of the United States sojourn may only be made after a student's return to Mexico, possibly many years after. In Chapter 5 some attempt will be made at such an evaluation. At this point it seems desirable to enter a note of interpretation and warning. If there is any reader who feels that the major objective of exchange programs is to secure wholehearted approval of the United States, he may consider that this chapter demonstrates the failure of the exchange process. Such a reader should reflect that the degree of success he postulates as desirable could have but one effect: the vast majority of Mexican students would choose to stay in the United States. Those who because of family or other ties found it impossible to do so would be disaffected and alienated from their own culture to such a degree as to render them ineffective interpreters of the United States and handicapped in transferring techniques to Mexico. While deferring further discussion, we wish to assert two things: first, that the exchange in most cases resulted in the acquisition or improvement of skills and techniques to a substantial degree; and secondly, that in a large majority of cases, understanding, friendship, and sympathy for the United States were increased even though there was selective rejection of some aspects of United States culture and policy.

Finally it may be observed that the areas in which the majority of our students were most favorably influenced during their stay in the United States are, by and large, areas in which Mexico is undergoing change and in which the students themselves felt they were changing even more rapidly than Mexico. The majority of the students favored political and social democracy and they approved of our successes in these areas and disapproved of our failures. The position of women is changing in Mexico and there is some loosening of family ties; consequently, although strong believers in the importance of the family, they approved of greater equality for women and less authoritarianism in the family structure.

Some of the students' reactions were conditioned by their social position and their beliefs about the home country. Those adhering most strongly to traditional values were the ones who least approved United States family life and the greater freedom for women and children. Those most committed to incorporating the Indian into Mexican society and diminishing class differences were the ones who were most apt to see the United States as a relatively classless society and also to be most critical of our treatment of the Negro. Those committed to the industrialization of Mexico were the most favorably inclined toward the United States economic system. To a noticeable degree, then, the ideological and sociocultural position of Mexico influenced the areas in which favorable student responses were most apt to occur and, as we will see, to be maintained after return.

Consequences and Problems

IN PRECEDING chapters we have considered the nature of Mexican culture, the origins and characteristics of Mexican students before coming to the United States, the experiences of Mexican students in the United States, and the changes undergone in a selected group of opinions and attitudes. To the extent that these changes persist and the student brings back and is able to use new knowledge and skills, cross-cultural education has consequences both for the home culture and for the individual. These we propose to examine in this chapter.

The student on his return is a different person from what he was when he left and ordinarily will occupy a new position within Mexican society. His pattern of personal relationships has been altered and his life chances are different. In a sense he is apt to be estranged from Mexican culture; at the very least he now is more conscious of it and sees it from a different perspective. Usually, and perhaps always, he will pass through a period of readjustment to the home culture, not unlike that which he experienced when he arrived in the United States.

A second category of consequences includes the effects of the returned student upon the home culture and society. To what extent does he employ his new knowledge and skill and how are they diffused through the society? What new roles does the student returnee occupy and what is his influence? To what degree does the returned student communicate his experiences to others and do his changed opinions and attitudes alter the general climate of opinion of the larger society or some restricted segment thereof? Our discussion of these and other consequences is highly tentative and inadequate. While we may infer a relationship between the changes in our students and subsequent changes in Mexican culture, demonstration would require a much longer and more intensive study.

In addition to considering the consequences of cross-cultural education, we will summarize some interpretations of the data with respect to the practical considerations of student exchange. We wish to reiterate that the purpose of the research was not to evaluate the success or failure of the exchange of students or to provide answers to the practical problems confronting the program administrator or foreign student adviser or the citizen who wishes to contribute to the success of exchange experiences. Nevertheless, some of the results of our research have implications for action. Lack of first-hand experience with action problems may cause us to overlook significant implications of our data, but it seems desirable for those who conducted the research to make such interpretations as they can.

ANTICIPATION OF RETURN

Other studies suggest that foreign students frequently experience strong apprehensions on the eve of their return to the home country. In many cases these apprehensions take the form of lowered morale and increased hostility toward the United States and the university. Our evidence suggests that this type of reaction was relatively mild among Mexican students when it occurred at all.

The evidence from written instruments and interviews indicates that the majority of the Mexican students in our sample had relatively realistic career goals. The interview materials especially show that the students had made a sober and realistic appraisal of what they might expect in the way of jobs and income. Some expected to enter family businesses; others expected to get through family connections similar or better jobs than they had held before. Some expected to gain prestige as a result of their better command of English and their educational experiences. Others were less optimistic.

Enrique Jiménez remarked: "Being a research worker at the present time in Mexico I would have to starve probably; the salary at the University is ridiculous, is miserable." His not unrealistic hope was to gain substantial recognition as a research worker in his field in the United States; rather clearly he hoped to emulate another research man in a related field who became sufficiently distinguished to be invited back to Mexico on his own terms as head of an adequate research institute. Others interested in teaching or research careers were similarly pessimistic. Few anticipated that on their return they would secure a job that would support a family; they anticipated having to take outside work in addition. None mentioned the problem of validation or acceptance of degrees from the United States. Nor was concern expressed over problems of personal and social readjustment on return to Mexico.

THE REALITIES OF RETURN

For some students the actualities of return presented much more severe problems than they had anticipated. Baldovinos and Pérez Castro cite as a reasonably typical experience that described in the following letter (in translation):

During the last two weeks of our stay in the University, we could not sleep for excitement, wakefully envisioning the longed-for return to the homeland. Never in my life have I felt such deep desires to get to work with every fiber, moved with great enthusiasm to cooperate, and disposed to dedicate my training to the cause of raising, even though it be on a small scale, the level of living of our agricultural families. How brutal then the shock of entering again into reality, so low and ignominious the actions of persons attached to the border customs post through which we entered the country concerning our introduction of a few domestic articles with more than two years use but classified "importation prohibited." After four days of listening to dishonest proposals we finished by throwing them in the river, my wife weeping bitterly at the abuse they wished to commit, and I returned to walk our soil full of bitterness and heartbroken. Afterwards: reception rooms, waits, evasions, promises, accusations of being a *malinchista* (when from the day I went abroad I felt more lively my affection for Mexico). They said to me I came to ask the "pearls of the Virgin" for working, jealous, because according to them "I was above myself" for having been abroad, and scornful of my concern for a decent salary, moved by imperious necessities. I returned with two children. I ended by resigning myself, returning temporarily to my previous employment until finally, after a year and a half, I began to work in a new situation with magnificent prospects.[1]

In their study of returned fellowship holders in agricultural sciences, Baldovinos and Pérez Castro do not consider problems of personal readjustment. Seventy-three per cent of their subjects, however, reported difficulties in applying their specialized training. Only 13.5 per cent said they had no difficulties and 13.5 per cent did not reply. Lack of facilities such as laboratories, libraries, and machinery were among the difficulties men-

[1] Baldovinos and Pérez Castro, *op. cit.*, pp. 70–71.

tioned by 55.6 per cent. Almost half (48.2 per cent) mentioned poor circumstances for work such as poor organization, bureaucracy, indifference, lack of interest and cooperation, and lack of understanding. Inadequate salaries were mentioned by 37.1 per cent. The authors likewise found that only two thirds of the returned fellows were directly or indirectly engaged in activities which made use of their training abroad in a form contributing to the development of Mexican agriculture. While poor selection may account for the fact that 34 per cent were not utilizing their training, the authors felt that the failure in most cases was due to discouragement and the lack of opportunity, representing a substantial loss on the investment of the agencies sponsoring fellowships. They suggested that, on the one hand, fellowships for foreign study should be regarded as the highest honors obtainable by students, and that, on the other, sponsoring agencies have a responsibility for the proper employment of the knowledge gained by the student during his study abroad.

To discuss the problems of returned students in fields other than the agricultural sciences and to examine problems of social adjustment and opinion and attitudes dimensions, we must turn to less systematic observations. Most of the comments in the remainder of this section are derived from a preliminary summary report prepared by Norman D. Humphrey for the Committee on Cross-Cultural Education, and from his article "The Mexican Image of Americans."[2] Both were checked with his field notebooks.

The problem of securing recognition for study in the United States varies significantly from one field to another and depending upon whether work is at the undergraduate or the graduate level. Undergraduates are apt to be frustrated or resentful because the bachelor's degree from the American university is equated with the *bachillerato*, a secondary school diploma. The situation is even more difficult where licensing provisions exist for professions or work taken abroad must be validated. These add to the resentments when such a degree as a B.S. in engineering is not considered equivalent to the Mexican title of *ingeniero*.

Somewhat the same situation exists at the graduate level although in some fields it is less acute. In many fields such a degree as the Ph.D. has no equivalent in Mexico. In these cases the degree usually receives full recognition. On the other hand, such degrees as D.D.S. will require valida-

[2] Norman D. Humphrey, "The Mexican Image of Americans," *Annals of the American Academy of Political and Social Science*, 295:116–25 (September 1954).

tion, involving fees, attendance at courses, or passing examinations. Bureaucratic red tape, fees, and the *mordida* apparently prevent most returned students from making the effort. One student spent 3000 pesos to validate an engineering degree, a sum equal to all the fees for the similar course in the National University. The least difficulty in utilizing and gaining recognition for American study is encountered by those who completed available training in Mexico and subsequently took additional training in the United States. This again is particularly true where licensing or validation procedures are required.

Returnees who have done undergraduate work in the United States or who have done advanced work in business administration and various economic and industrial specialties are apt to seek employment in some American business firm. Here they encounter frustration and develop resentments because they usually receive lower salaries than American counterparts in the organization. On the job they must hide anti-American sentiments and critical attitudes. Once outside the framework of his job, the returnee must disguise his Americanization and he finds that relations with his friends, sponsors, and similar influence groups have been curtailed. If he is in a government job he is "tested" by jealous colleagues both professionally and for his ideas. Especially the student who has done graduate work is constantly subjected to accusations of being a *Malinchista* or of being *agringado* or even of being a *pocho*. (The three terms refer respectively to: (1) considering foreign things superior to Mexican; (2) having become like a *gringo*; (3) having lived in the United States so long that one speaks or behaves like a Mexican-American. The latter term is especially derogatory because it is usually applied to lower-class persons.)

Usually returnees do not find themselves occupying as important roles as they anticipated nor do they achieve the prestige they expected. Students tend to feel slightly defrauded and to ascribe this to their foreign experience. Resentments are hence apt to be directed toward the United States. Frequently there is some estrangement from the student's family. Not infrequently the family attributes changes to the foreign study, whereas the returnee attributes these to maturation. Usually the students' basic attitudes have undergone changes that contribute to the difficulty of reestablishing social relationships.

Exceptions to this situation occur in a significant number of cases. Some returned students described experiences similar to those contained in the letter quoted on page 101, but the reaction is without bitterness. Significantly these students had anticipated a period of adjustment and establishment of connections in Mexico: hence they apparently took the initial difficulties in stride. Moreover, job adjustment is frequently much more satisfactory than in the cases described, especially where the superior officer has also studied in the United States, where a substantial number of fellow employees have studied in the United States, or where the job is one for which few or no Mexican-trained personnel exist. Nevertheless the envy and suspicion with which the returned student is regarded both on and off the job usually cause him to become a strong cultural nationalist in order to avoid criticism.

Pro-Americanism or being suspected of *malinchismo* are definite political liabilities and few returned students engage directly in politics. Nevertheless many of the desirable jobs for returnees are in the government bureaucracy. Even here enemies or jealous colleagues are quick to make public accusations if a man is too hospitable to American visitors or too cordial to American colleagues. (This may occur even if a man has never studied in the United States.) Assistance to Protestant groups is especially dangerous; one man lost his job for aiding a Protestant group in a purely educational undertaking. Hence returnees again are apt to be overtly anti-American and any political activity consists of participation in occupational associations that influence the government.

In general, attitudes toward the United States are more favorable among older persons who studied in the United States before the increase in nationalism of recent years, or who are not threatened in job or career possibilities, or who have other supportive relationships. Supportive relationships are formed when numerous colleagues or several members of the family have also studied in the United States. This is more apt to occur among families which are part of the older aristocracy rather than among the relatively new upward-aspiring middle class.

Even so, returned students are apt to show a rather heightened sensitivity toward American cultural penetration and political or economic domination. Such attitudes must be seen in the context of the history of United States–Mexico relations which creates far greater apprehensions than seems realistic to many North Americans. At one extreme, a distinguished returned student privately expressed belief in the ultimate political absorption of Mexico by the United States, an event which he felt he must work personally to delay as long as possible. Yet despite the existence of such sentiments, strongest among professional and intellectual groups, returnees often maintain close and cordial relations with North American colleagues and maintain ties with professional societies in the United States. Joint meetings with North American professional or scholarly societies and international meetings at which North Americans are the most numerous foreign attendants have increased considerably in recent years.

On a more personal level the returned student is uplifted and full of idealistic notions of what he can do for Mexico. Frequently he finds himself constrained by antagonisms, restrictions upon opportunity, and often by involvement in routine bureaucratic tasks or in the difficult struggle to earn enough money to keep up the standard of living he now considers proper. He becomes more sensitive to the less desirable aspects of Mexican life, although at the same time he may resent criticism by North Americans even more than before. As one said, he "became both more and less nationalistic." If difficulties and disappointments are great, he often seeks support and comfort in the privacy and security provided by the primary group of family and kindred, despite the controls the primary group exerts and his heightened conflict with it.

On the positive side, the returnee is apt to remember with some nostalgia the easy, friendly atmosphere of the United States and the new understanding of family and personal relationships he acquired while a student. Several of the best adjusted share the feelings of one who described his college experience as "the best years of my life." But hard work, language difficulties, loneliness, and a sense of rejection are among the dominant memories of others, surely under-represented in our data because of Mexican politeness and the unrepresentativeness of the sample. Nevertheless the returnee usually bears with him some new ethical concepts and notions of punctuality, cleanliness, order, and responsibility which in some measure set him apart from his fellows. In several areas, most returned students seem to have undergone permanent shifts in their personal value structures, shifts that tend to affect their behavior in a wide variety of situations. The most common and important changes seem to be toward greater egalitarianism, increased cooperativeness, greater open-mindedness, and more feelings of social responsibility.

In some cases returnees are conscious of these shifts and can verbalize them. In other cases they may be inferred either from the structure of personal faith, from shifts in occupation, or from differences in the behaviors of the returnee in relation to his primary groups or to larger institutions. The general areas of change are similar to those in which the students in the United States also show the greatest differences from traditional Mexican values and it may be argued that they represent predispositions to study in the United States rather than the effects of study in this country. It is a limitation of the present study that this question cannot be answered definitively.

On the other hand there does seem to be a relation between the degree of change in the returned students and such factors as the length of residence in the United States, the intensity of participation in American life, and the degree of favorableness felt toward the United States. The extent of difference or change is more apparent among individuals with cosmopolitan family backgrounds or persons who are otherwise so situated that they do not feel the need publicly to renounce American influences upon their return. It is true that the higher the class position of the returnee, the greater his concern with the spiritual values of Mexican life. But again it is precisely in this sphere that students in the United States showed themselves to be almost wholly traditional. It would seem likely, therefore, that we are dealing with areas of genuine and permanent change.

The ways in which changes are manifested obviously vary from individual to individual but we may identify some fairly common characteristics. For example, idealism and socio-centrism usually are increased. *Egoismo* loses some of its hold and the ability to admit ignorance and to tolerate conflicting opinions increases. Efficiency, orderliness, systematization, and punctuality all come to be more valued. Emotional support for the improvement of public education increases. Increased cooperativeness in government enterprises is proportional to the amount of graduate work in the United States.

Interpersonal relations become less formal. In general there is a curtailment of impulsiveness and a greater calculation of the risks of undertakings. And when obligations and duties are assumed, they are carried out.

Greater independence of judgment and less reliance upon authority are directly related to the degree of the student's Americanization. Students who changed in these respects are less concerned with "changing only with the group." Toleration of religious differences increases with increased length of stay in the United States. Many students reported that the United States experience helped them to see Mexico more clearly — not only were they able to criticize its faults more objectively but they

106

developed deeper awareness of and love for the distinctive aspects of Mexican life, the landscapes, the street sounds, the cries of street vendors, the music, the smell of roasting coffee, the odor of roasting corn. Some reported a greater identification with people in all walks of life; as one said "even the beggars became old friends." At the same time, those with increased awareness and identification were impelled to criticize and to urge improvements, which opened them to charges of *malinchismo*.

Increased egalitarianism is manifest primarily in family life and is related to the intensity of participation in American life. Usually there is greater permissiveness in child rearing. The husbands tend to participate more actively in child rearing rather than remaining remote figures of authority. The self-esteem of wives is enhanced in various ways. They more frequently participate in decision-making. American friends of the husband may be entertained in the home and wives are included in a wider range of social events. The inner rebellion against the traditional family authority of the father is magnified. Changes in women returnees are similar but much more marked.

That this egalitarianism represents a true change is suggested by the unhappiness of individuals who, through circumstances, have been forced to re-enter fully into a traditional family relationship. As an extreme example we may cite the case of a returned student whose eighty-year-old father was still head of the extended family. When this student was interviewed he was forty-five. He lived at home and worked in a family business rather than practicing journalism which he had studied in the United States. Not only could he make no important decisions but he had to seek permission before inviting a nonrelative to the house.

Several returnees indicated that American family life was the principal area in which they defended the United States and sought to correct the impressions of their friends and associates. In this connection some argued that American tourists should not be taken as indicative of American attitudes and behaviors, both because they are not representative and because they are people momentarily outside the restraints of their own culture. Some commented that they thought tourists' behavior had improved in recent years and that a larger percentage attempted to speak Spanish and learn about Mexico sympathetically. One gave detailed reasons why the American business colony in Mexico is also unrepresentative; not only does it isolate itself from Mexican life but it reinforces Mexican stereotypes by excessive emphasis upon material goals.

Except for those employed by American firms, relatively few returnees have contacts with Americans resident in Mexico. Some have significant associations with other returnees, especially in their own fields or among relatives. People in technical, professional, and teaching fields maintain, as we have said, their major contacts with the United States through membership in professional organizations, and subscriptions to professional, technical, and popular magazines, and through American visitors in their own fields.

So far as our data are representative then, there is strong indication that returned students are substantially different from other Mexicans and that these differences are at least in part related to the duration of the student's stay, the intensity of his participation in American life, and in some cases the student's age at the time of the stay. Favorableness toward the United States exerts some effect but is harder to disentangle from circumstances after return that may require protective behavior. Quite probably the intervening opportunities to utilize effectively or capitalize upon the United States experience may also influence the persistence of the changes and the extent to which they are communicated beyond the individual.

Estimates of the career value of the United States experience by most returnees tended to be relatively neutral or negative. Unless they had studied in the United States subjects for which no training facilities existed in Mexico, the majority felt that they could have secured as good training at home and many felt they would be further along in their chosen fields if they had not studied abroad. The major explanation for this feeling was the loss of contacts with persons of "influence" who could have advanced their careers, or the loss of time spent abroad when their fellows were already at work. This was less true of those who had studied at advanced levels or got highly specialized training.

Criticisms of the educational aspect of the United States experience were nevertheless quite contradictory. On the one hand, some emphasized the narrow specialization of United States training. A biologist, for example, felt that the United States–trained student received less general training in biology than students in Mexico and was deficient in knowledge both of the philosophy of science in general and of biology in particular. On the other hand, some complained that training was too general and without direct relevance to Mexican problems. A man in public health, for example, complained strongly about having to write a paper on public health problems in India. How, he asked, would this help him to solve problems in Mexico? The feelings of a majority of the returnees interviewed fell between these extremes.

A higher percentage mentioned that their better command of English after their stay in the United States had been a real aid in their work or careers. A few considered it a major factor in whatever success they had achieved.

Surprisingly few returnees on direct questioning felt they had received any intangible benefits from their experience; they had no sense of increased "social capital." Yet the majority indirectly revealed such benefits in the course of their interviews. Their greater understanding of Mexico has been mentioned already. Many also mentioned a general broadening of their view: they felt they understood better not only the United States but the world. Although few came to feel, as did one man, "a citizen of the world," most showed evidence that on many subjects their horizons no longer were limited to Mexico. And several mentioned greater adaptability and maturity as positive gains.

In interviews returnees probably tended to stress unfavorable aspects of their experience — indeed they were encouraged to do so. However, one returnee, who had emphasized the hostility and suspicion of his colleagues, later mentioned that younger men in his office had questioned him at length and as a result three had sought and obtained fellowships to study in the United States. A few others also mentioned similar experiences and some remarked rather casually that they were either planning for their children to study in the United States or hoped that they would. Indirect evidence thus suggests that a larger percentage of returnees experienced intellectual, social, or emotional rewards than the answers to direct questions indicate.

THE STUDENT AND CULTURE CHANGE

This monograph is, as we have indicated, dedicated to using the cultural approach in studying the exchange of students. The first chapter explored provisionally the major cultural characteristics of the urban middle and upper class from which most students come. In subsequent chapters an attempt was made to describe student backgrounds and their experiences in the United States, at least partially in cultural terms. Changes in attitudes and opinions, for example, were in some measure cast in a framework of cultural themes or values and social relationships and institutions.

In this final chapter it is relevant to ask whether we can describe the outcome or consequences of Mexican study in the United States in terms of culture change and culture contact or acculturation. Thus far we have attempted to relate the behavior of the Mexican student to his cultural background on the one hand and his contact with the culture of the United States on the other. From what we have tentatively established about the effects of the American experience upon the student, can we now generalize concerning the consequences for Mexican culture?

Theoretical, methodological, and substantive inadequacies place limitations upon the approach. The theoretical framework of culture contact or acculturation, which should be the most relevant to our purposes, is clearly at a relatively undeveloped level. Methods of studying whole cultures are still unsatisfactory, the more so when research deals with a complex of subcultures such as Mexico presents. Finally, some of the tools of social science have yet to be applied in Mexico. Hence our conclusions are largely intuitive.

The attempt to isolate the effects upon culture change of a special class of individuals such as the foreign student adds to our difficulties. We may assume that Mexico has an inner dynamic of culture change; nevertheless, much of the change observable today is heavily affected by outside contacts and influences, especially from Europe and the United States. The permeability of the United States–Mexican border affects much more than the student group. From among the effects of mass communications, hundreds of thousands of American tourists, thousands of permanent or semi-permanent American residents in Mexico, an enormous commercial interchange, and the return of some millions of Mexican visitors from the United States, isolating the effect of a few thousand Mexican students is a forbidding task indeed.

In the terminology employed by the Social Science Research Council Seminar on Acculturation,[3] Mexico may be characterized as an autonomous sociocultural system with nationalism providing the major boundary-maintaining mechanism. Nationalism is reinforced with respect to the United States, by the language difference and by the concept of *la raza*. The latter is a more or less self-conscious and coherent set of values and perceptions which, in the larger sense, sets off countries with a Latin Catholic tradition from countries with an Anglo-Saxon Protestant tradi-

[3] "Acculturation: An Exploratory Formulation," *American Anthropologist*, 56:973–1002 (December 1954).

tion. Specifically Mexican values and perceptions exist, but only a few need be identified for the purpose of this analysis.

Since independence, and especially since 1910, the Mexican sociocultural system has been to some extent selectively flexible or open. Extension of democratic and egalitarian values, mass education, technological innovation (including administrative innovations), and industrialization today are, in varying degrees, it is true, fairly widely accepted areas of openness among most strata of Mexican society. (They often are meaningless, of course, in some of the "enclave" or "parallel" Indian societies.) The system is rigid and closed, especially in the urban middle and upper class, with respect to preservation of the importance of the family and the "spiritual" and humanistic values relating to ultimate life goals and closely associated with both the Latin cultural tradition and Catholic values. (The North American unfamiliar with anti-clericalism should be reminded that even the most fervent anti-clerical Mexican usually is a supporter of what he believes to be the Catholic faith and the Catholic value system.)

Insofar as the Mexican attitude toward acculturation is conscious, it is an attempt to seize and amalgamate the "best of both ways." Thus, industrialization and capitalism are to be "controlled" to avoid the evils Mexicans see attending these phenomena in the United States. The interrelated character of elements within a culture is seldom appreciated and the possible relation of the Protestant ethic or of attitudes toward work to industrial development is not discussed. The Mexican goal, then, is some type of syncretism, leading neither to fusion nor assimilation, but rather to some dynamic equilibrium with the culture of the United States.

Internal conflict arising out of the stresses created by culture contact in Mexico today is primarily in terms, not of goals, but of the degree and rapidity of change to be accepted. "Nativistic" reactions still exist among the more traditional but are not the source of significant conflicts. Continuing adjustment to a progressive economy and the creation of new social and cultural forms are widely accepted Mexican goals whose different interpretations generate most conflicts.

As an agent of acculturation, the Mexican student is the bearer of only part of United States culture. The extent of his learning is conditioned partly by his experiences and length of stay, partly by his intrinsic curiosity and interest. In any case, his knowledge is segmental and of three levels of intensity. A certain part of United States culture he experiences direct-

111

ly through participation. Another part he observes, but does not directly participate in. A third he hears or reads about but neither observes nor experiences. And part he learns nothing about.

He participates most intensely in the university subculture; this he may learn rather completely. Living experiences familiarize him with many material aspects of United States culture; he observes or hears about many more. He may observe or hear about the productivity of labor and differing attitudes toward labor, but, unless he takes a job, he rarely has experience of them. He hears about, and may observe, racial discrimination but rarely experiences it. In political life, he may observe the functioning of the civil bureaucracy, the conduct of elections, and the orderly transfer of power, but he rarely penetrates to any details of the political process. His historical knowledge of the culture is slight. At the attitude, opinion, and value level, his knowledge is unsystematic, often basically accidental in character. This list is illustrative only but serves perhaps to indicate the limited nature of the student's knowledge.

On his return, the student is an important bearer of new technical skills, and his role in furthering such goals as political and social democracy and improved living standards is reinforced. Often he becomes at the same time a more self-conscious defender of humanistic and spiritual values of his own culture and seeks to support such boundary-maintaining mechanisms as nationalism. Because he has in a sense "looked upon the face of evil," he must reaffirm his faith in the basic Mexican values supported by his class.

This reaffirmation becomes the more necessary because hundreds of thousands of returned workers have been seduced by the materialistic values of the United States. Loyalty to the spiritual aspects of the Mexican value system has little appeal to men impressed with the greater order, security, and access to material goods enjoyed by the worker in the United States. Articulate opposition to the movement of Mexican labor to the United States increasingly stresses the undesirable Americanization of the returned worker.

Two roles are thus defined for the returnee. On the one hand he is an agent of culture contact, the transmitter of desired technical skills and more democratic values. At the same time, his cross-cultural experience has usually made him more perceptive of cultural differences and, both as a protective device and as a result of his social class, he often becomes an articulate supporter of core Mexican values and a defender of boundary-maintaining mechanisms. Not surprisingly, unless these conflicting cultural roles can be compartmentalized, the lot of the individual is not a happy one. Yet it is in playing these two roles that the returned student is most apt to achieve the social position that may make him the most effective agent of culture contact.

The reader who sees in student exchange a means of promoting friendship and international understanding may be somewhat dismayed at the constant reference to anti-American sentiments among returned students. We would remind such readers again that most students who have spent much time in the United States are selective in their appraisal of this country. Frequently they have gained great understanding and their criticism is often, in their own eyes, friendly and constructive. In the historically conditioned climate of opinion in Mexico the returned student is forced to display overt anti-Americanism which frequently he does not feel. Likewise it must be recognized that given the existing climate, the individual who exhibits a carefully gauged amount of anti-Americanism may be in a far better position to transmit the influence of his training in the United States and the modifications which have occurred in his outlook than would be the returnee who arouses hostility by his unreserved friendship and admiration for the United States.

There are, of course, alternative targets for antagonism. The long-standing prejudices in Mexico against the Spanish have been exacerbated by the Spanish civil war and many segments of Mexican society are far more antagonistic to Spain than to the United States. Thus an unpublished study of two issues of *Todo*, a "slick paper" magazine, by Raoul Naroll disclosed repeated and unrestrained anti-Spanish prejudice. At the same time anti-American sentiment was completely absent. Most references to the United States were neutral so far as affect was concerned. And an issue containing a violent polemic against the importation of Spanish bull fighters also contained a completely objective account of the Pershing expedition of 1916, regarded by most Mexicans as a completely unwarranted flouting of Mexican sovereignty.

Having alternative objects of dislike, however, may be two-edged; for many Mexicans any United States overtures toward the Franco government in Spain result in the transference of their hostility to this country. Naroll indeed argues that the whole anti-Spanish attitude is a case of displaced hostility against the United States. Another example may be to the point. Some of the strongest opposition to Communism is among intel-

113

lectuals and in upper-class circles, especially those with a strong clerical bias, who are also the most anti-American. As a result we find a strongly anti-American group supporting United States foreign policy insofar as the Communist issue is concerned. The effects of alternative targets for hostility upon individual and group attitudes deserves further research by social scientists, for the problem has relevance beyond its implications for this study.

To recapitulate, our data show that returned students have transmitted technical skills and knowledge which resulted in innovations in their culture. These have been most clear in business and industry — in both production and administration — and least effective in government. In education they have been most effective in the sciences (including some of the social sciences), least effective or nil in the humanities. In areas such as policy formation, social change, public opinions and attitudes, and value shifts, the evidence is mainly indirect.

It is probable that such governmental changes as the introduction of the graduated income tax and the development of the law of trusteeship are the result of culture contact; without case histories of such innovations, we cannot be sure what part, if any, returned students played in them, although certainly some students must have returned with knowledge of their operation in the United States. Trends toward governmental efficiency, greater political democracy, and expanded education receive support from returned students but we cannot isolate their contribution as innovators. Within their social class group with few exceptions, returned students will be in advance of general trends in Mexican society toward greater egalitarianism, whether this is in less authoritarian family relationships, greater equality for women, or higher living standards for the underprivileged. They will be strong supporters of those aspects of nationalism related to its function in maintaining the cultural boundary for the preservation of the individuality and the spiritual values of Mexican culture, but few will be in decision-making positions.

In acculturational terms, the student group tends to support and contribute to the openness of Mexican culture to cultural influences from the United States and the western urban-industrial pattern but to strive consciously for syncretism rather than assimilation. Hence they also support boundary-preserving mechanisms they believe will ensure the autonomy of the cultural system. With respect to these and other aspects in which the student may have been affected by his United States experience, we have no measure of the relative importance and influence of the returnee as compared with other possible avenues of influence. We can say, however, that the returned students occupy class and status positions which are influential and that, particularly in the field of social behavior, they tend to set norms and goals for the culture. In their performance of their class and status roles, they tend to be somewhat in advance of the direction in which the Mexican culture and society as a whole appears to be moving. Only more detailed studies of specific changes can reveal the relative importance of the returned student as an agent of culture contact.

IMPLICATIONS FOR EXCHANGE PROGRAMS

In this final section we present our reflections on the bearing of our data on programs for the exchange of students at the university level. Determination of the effects of the visit to the United States begins with selection. Little can be done about the self-financed majority of Mexican students, but some considerations appear applicable to those receiving fellowships from private or government agencies.

The objective of the selecting agency may affect the selection procedures but no single formula will suffice for all situations. If the primary objective is broadly speaking professional or technical, there will be variations in the type and length of training available in Mexico. Particularly where there are problems of licensing or recognition of foreign training or degrees, probably the most effective procedure is to select persons to receive specialized or additional training in the United States who have received substantially all the training possible in Mexico.

In fields where United States degrees are acceptable and for individuals going into business or interested simply in a humanistic education, training may begin earlier. It should be borne in mind, however, that young undergraduate students are apt to suffer more disruption of their friendship groups and to have greater difficulty in maintaining their social ties in Mexico. Consideration may well be given to the opportunities and facilities which the student will have to make use of his training after return. Little profit will accrue from training if there is slight prospect of a job in which the student can use it or, in the case of highly specialized training, if he will not find proper laboratory, library, and other facilities on his return. The responsibilities of the selecting agency should not end with the selection and award but should include some follow-up while the student is in the United States and after his return to Mexico.

If the objective of the program is the creation of binational understanding or some vaguely formulated concept of good will, it is doubtful if an adequate basis for selection can be made. Our evidence suggests that the most good will accrues from programs which are strictly educational in objective, which provide the Mexican student with training and information he needs and is able to apply successfully on his return. In these cases understanding and good will may be by-products of the experience. Our data suggest, however, that many people receiving highly technical training are relatively indifferent to other aspects of their experience in the United States and even if they arrive and leave with a great store of good will for this country, they frequently acquire very little understanding of it.

In this connection, it may be observed that students at undergraduate age levels are apt to be more impressionable and are more likely to have their attitudes and opinions modified while in the United States than are older students. However, it is possible that they are more frustrated on their return because of destruction of friendship groups and that their new attitudes and opinions are modified as easily as they were acquired. In all types of cases, however, there seems to be some relation between the length of stay in the United States and the growth of understanding, the extent of modification of attitudes and opinions, and the degree to which these are internalized and become permanent. The danger of alienation because of long stays seems less in the case of Mexican students than for other nationalities. At least this seems true so far as the temptation to stay in the United States is concerned; we have little information to evaluate the degree of alienation from the home culture on return.

For some types of training programs the regional or class origins of individuals may be important. Middle- or upper-class origins and university degrees are not apt to produce returnees who will work in the field or the factory. They may, if they want to do research, be drawn to the laboratory, but they will have strong drives to obtain administrative jobs in urban settings. Similarly, individuals from highly urban backgrounds are far less apt to operate effectively in rural or less developed areas. The fact that we encountered few students from heavily populated southern Mexico and virtually none from the most important agricultural areas of the plateau perhaps has important implications for program planning.

A limiting factor in planning completely satisfactory programs is of course the availability of people with adequate qualifications. Most discussions of foreign students emphasize their need for better language training and tend to make linguistic ability the primary criterion for selection. Strong, but not conclusive, evidence suggests that while adequate linguistic background is a help, such factors as preparation for the work to be done in the United States, motivation, length of stay in the United States, and assurance of a job on return are at least as important in predicting the success of students as is language ability.

Orientation programs apparently can help the foreign student, but, as we have indicated, they are perhaps less important for the Mexican student than for those from other countries. Orientation programs almost of necessity create protected situations in which the student is provided with better housing, more social activity, and a greater sense of importance than he will experience in his later university or college stay. This situation may create disappointments unless the program includes some explicit discussion of differences the students may expect when they reach the university. Students generally feel that they should have more realistic briefing on the nature of the American university, its requirements, its competitiveness, and its grading system.

The fact that virtually all Mexican students mention language as the source of their principal difficulty, even for those who had passed screening examinations, suggests that for Mexican students orientation programs might most profitably be organized about a six weeks' to two months' intensive language program before the start of classwork in the university. By proper organization of reading material and class discussion most of the other functions of orientation programs could be carried out simultaneously.

Another need is to make the students intelligently aware of problems of cultural diversity or cultural relativism. One value mentioned by students is their increasing awareness and understanding of their own culture and greater knowledge of cultural differences in other parts of the world as a result of their experience in the United States. Practically no students arrive with any real sense of the nature of cultural differences and it would appear to be useful to make them conscious of these differences. Such preparation should increase their understanding and acceptance of cultural differences and might help to reduce value conflicts that occur when students come upon such differences unprepared.[4] The fact that so many

[4] This point is elaborated by C. A. D. van Nienwenhuijze of the Institute for Social Studies, The Hague, in a manuscript on cross-cultural education he expects to publish soon. "Participants," he writes, "come in as laymen in the very thing that confronts

students do not come on sponsored programs suggests that for universities with large foreign student populations, orientation programs might be established at the university.

When the student reaches the university or college where he is to study, he will today commonly find a special adviser and in large institutions a more or less well staffed and trained foreign student adviser's office. We assume that there is general recognition of the desirability of organized aid to the foreign student in finding housing and caring for his health and welfare, but frequently neither the foreign student nor the institution is prepared to cope with catastrophic illness or accident. But even in universities with the best organized foreign student offices, certain limitations appear common.

Arbitrary bureaucratic responses to students' problems apparently are frequent outside the foreign student adviser's office. Mexican students come with great personal pride and confidence both in their background and in their abilities, a confidence that evidence suggests is justified in most cases. They are antagonized by administrators' failure to interpret their credentials properly and resentful when they find they cannot immediately take the kinds of courses they anticipated or are, in their view, unduly limited in their program. Lucid exposition of the limitations of the American university, the nature of its requirements, and differences in methods of instruction often can make it clear that restrictions on programs are not a reflection upon the individual or his background. Explanation of alternative ways of meeting requirements would often aid students in tailoring their programs more closely to their needs.

The provision of alternative goals often may greatly diminish disappointments if students cannot complete degree requirements. A formal Certificate of Study, resembling a diploma and specifying the duration and the field of study, has recently been adopted by the University of California for foreign students who cannot remain long enough to secure a degree. It appears to meet many genuine needs satisfactorily. Certificates are granted only on departmental recommendation for work meeting the same grade standards as those required for degrees.

---

them all on account of their coming together. They are supposed to concentrate on something else. In other words, they are meant to remain laymen in the matter upon which a good deal of the result of their meeting depends." And again, "It is not at all impossible that further research may yield the conclusion that, regardless of subject matter, attention must be paid in any cross-cultural project to what is, in the given project, the actual meaning of cultural diversity."

As we have indicated, the Mexicans' difficulties in social adjustment are probably considerably less than those of many other foreign student groups. The Mexican student could benefit from assistance in this field but he is not apt to be very responsive to group social activities or satisfied with them unless they lead to his rapid absorption by American student groups. He does not want to form part of a foreign student culture or a Latin American student culture or a Mexican student culture. Rather his interests are in becoming a participating member of the general American student environment. Most particularly he is antagonistic toward what our colleague, Harry Hoijer, calls the "Oh-so-quaint" approach to exotic cultures. The type of gathering where various foreign students wear picturesque "native" costumes and answer the uninformed even though well-meaning questions of Americans has no attraction for him. For our urban male student of the upper-middle or upper class the appropriate common native costume is a well-tailored business suit.

The Mexican student does wish greater personal contact with both professors and students. His frequently voiced disappointment is that he has seen so little of American family and home life. This complaint comes a little strangely from the Mexican student who in his own country usually invites only his most intimate associates into his home.

Desirable effects in the student also accrue from opportunities to know people of differing class and occupational status. Despite the students' generally negative attitudes toward organized activities, tours through the local region during holidays apparently are enjoyed and produce good effects. The students' main complaint usually is that they get weary of hearing everything described as the biggest and the best by Americans who naively assume either that similar things do not exist in the student's home country or that they could automatically be transferred there. Students probably would react best to discussions of problems that have been faced and the way that they have been or are being met, whether the subject is agriculture, industry, or social relationships.

Administrative officers and faculties who must deal with the personal problems and attitudes of Mexican students will find it helpful to bear in mind that many acute conflict situations have their roots in the home country and are apt to stem from difficulties with their families created by students' changing ideological position. The great strength of Mexican family ties make such conflicts unusually important for them. The effects of differing lengths of stay and the students' position in the probable adjustment cycle also illumine both their problems and their attitudes. The response of the student to his environment will vary considerably depending upon whether he is in the initial spectator phase, or having difficulties adjusting to the newly discovered complexities of American and university life, or has come to terms with his environment.

In the period before the student returns, it is well to remember, apprehensions may mount and be reflected again in personal disturbances and hostile attitudes. It has been suggested that orientation programs shortly before return might be as much or even more useful than at the beginning of the sojourn. Special programs for Mexican students are obviously impossible, but some generalized program is conceivable for students from a variety of countries. Such a program might help in organizing the experiences the student has had and prepare him for the kinds of readjustment problems he will face on his return. Here again the emphasis might well be on the meaning and understanding of cultural diversity. He might be prepared for encountering indifference or hostility or envy, for some degree of estrangement from his family and associates, and for the fact that he may not automatically improve his economic and social position immediately on his arrival home.

Apparently very little consideration has been given to the problem of the returned student. For those not involved in a fellowship program it is difficult to envision organized follow-through although individual universities either through the administration or possibly through alumni organizations might set up machinery for maintaining some contact. Some universities have alumni clubs abroad but there is a question whether these may not set the student further apart from his own culture. Certainly the ordinary procedures of maintaining contact with alumni are not adequate.

Students on fellowship programs perhaps could be followed up more effectively than others. Agencies carrying on such programs apparently rarely feel any responsibility for the student after return. Probably it would be impossible for an agency from outside the country to do much about job opportunities for the utilization of knowledge gained abroad. On the other hand, things could be done to better the working facilities of many former fellowship holders. It should be possible to maintain the returnee's contact with the United States to some degree by aiding him to develop his professional library, to maintain membership in professional societies, to subscribe to professional journals, and even perhaps to attend an occasional professional meeting.

In particular, apparently little thought has been given to the possibilities of refresher visits. It has been assumed that it is better to spread fellowship funds to as many individuals as possible rather than to encourage the fullest development of those who do receive fellowships. In many cases the student on first returning to his home country does not occupy a position of status and is in no position to apply much that he has learned abroad. If he succeeds in his chosen field, a period beginning five or ten years after he has been in the United States may be the most effective time for him to influence his technical field or profession. By this time his contacts with the United States are somewhat remote, he is no longer abreast of this country's developments in his field, and he may even have lost his enthusiasm for them. It might well be that bringing mature people back for visits five or ten years after they have held fellowships in the United States would increase the effectiveness of training many times.

Most of our remarks in this section have dealt with the professional and technical objectives of student exchange and we have said little about the values many see in such programs for improved understanding and friendship. We have suggested that these should be by-products of a sound educational program rather than a primary objective. Despite the difficulties students encounter in such programs, despite the fact that they tend to go home with somewhat critical and in some sense hostile attitudes toward the United States, the students themselves have little doubt as to the value of educational exchange. One of our most articulate students, after a session in which he had been rather critical of the United States, was asked what was the best way of improving United States–Mexican relations. He responded promptly, "Have more student exchanges." In other words, despite the fact that student exchange has many unsatisfactory aspects, it still remains one of the most effective ways of creating understanding and friendship and maintaining contacts between cultures.

Appendix and Index

Appendix

THE body of this report is devoted primarily to the presentation of research findings and gives relatively little information concerning the sources of data and the methods of data collection. This appendix is designed to permit the inquiring reader to make some evaluation of the conclusions and to aid future researchers interested in foreign students.

When the study of Mexican students was undertaken as one of the initial group of studies sponsored by the Committee on Cross-Cultural Education of the Social Science Research Council, little research on foreign students had been published. The applicability of rigorous quantitative methods to unknown cross-cultural situations was in doubt. Little knowledge existed concerning the range and relative importance of problems. Consequently, in this study, as in some of the other initial studies in this series, primary emphasis was placed upon extended interviewing and upon selecting investigators with substantial knowledge of the cultures of the students studied. In addition the part of the study concerned with Mexican students in the United States — the "domestic" study — experimented with the use of questionnaires and schedules. These are discussed later.

THE SAMPLE AND THE DATA COLLECTION METHODS

The part of this report concerned with Mexican students in the United States is based primarily upon open-ended interviews with a "core" group of nine regular full-time students and one Extension Division student enrolled at the University of California at Los Angeles. All but three were technically graduate students (two of the graduate students actually were taking undergraduate courses and one was a post-M.D. student). Six had studied at other institutions in the United States before enrolling at UCLA, and one graduate student had done undergraduate work at UCLA on a previous visit.

Interviews were conducted by Ralph Arellano and Lewis Stone. Students with the greatest linguistic difficulty were interviewed by Mr. Are-

125

llano, himself of Mexican ancestry, and were permitted to use either English or Spanish as they wished. Formal interviews were machine recorded in sessions of from one to two hours duration and later transcribed. The length of the interviews in some cases was limited, either because of lack of cooperation or, usually, because the students were extremely busy; but total formal interviews with each subject ranged from a minimum of about four hours for one student to from eight to over twenty hours for the others. In addition, interviewers met the subjects informally both off and on the campus. A simplified interview guide, based on that developed by William H. Sewell and associates for the Scandinavian project at the University of Wisconsin, was employed by the interviewers but students were encouraged to talk freely and spontaneously about whatever interested them. After transcription, the interview materials were grouped into fairly broad subject categories and analyzed for content and significance.

Because of the small number of "core" students, written background information and test materials were collected in 1952–53 from members of the core group and from twenty-two other students at Los Angeles State College, Los Angeles City College, the University of Southern California, and the University of California at Berkeley. In 1953–54 background information was secured from twenty additional subjects. Most of these same students also supplied written test materials (described later). The distribution of all students supplying information in both years follows:

	No.
UCLA	14
University of Southern California	11
University of California, Berkeley	9
Los Angeles City College	6
Los Angeles State College	4
University of Pennsylvania	4
University of Wisconsin	3
Louisiana State University	1
Total	52

The domestic study rests then upon background data from about 4.4 per cent of the Mexican students in the United States in 1952–53 (the percentage would be higher if European quota immigrants could be excluded), upon written test materials from a somewhat smaller percentage, and upon interviews with ten students. The latter, at UCLA, represented the available students at a particular time. Data from other students were obtained either through personal contacts with staff members (in the Los Angeles area) or through some person on a given campus who was willing either to get in touch with students or to supply a list of names and addresses. In the latter case forms were sent with letters to which slightly fewer than half replied. In other words, our information is from those individuals we could locate who were willing to or could be induced to cooperate.

In view of the lack of prior validation of the instruments, and the unsystematic character of the sample and of the methods of securing data, written instruments were not given a full statistical analysis. But some statistical comparisons of test data collected in 1952–53 with data collected in 1953–54 indicated no significant differences between the two groups. Moreover, the limited statistical results, conclusions drawn from interviews, and the basic characteristics of Mexican culture are highly consistent with one another. Additional confirmation was given by Norman D. Humphrey's conclusions independently derived from his interviews in Mexico.

The study of returned students in Mexico was made by Dr. Humphrey in 1952–53 in Mexico City and Guadalajara (the second largest city of Mexico). Contact was made with 71 returned students. From these, 26 case histories of varying lengths were secured, 22 from men and 4 from women. Of these, 11 might be classed as "intensive" case histories, including 9 from men and 2 from women.

As is characteristic of Mexicans, few persons refused outright to cooperate, but many evaded giving information either by failing to keep appointments, failing to set a time for interviewing, or discussing foreign students in general but not giving personal experiences. In a great many cases, the subjects held two or more jobs; hence time often was a real problem and frequently interviews were possible only at night. As in the domestic study, the interviews by Dr. Humphrey were with returned students who could be located, who had time, and who were willing to be interviewed. Both in Mexico and the United States suspicion of the purposes of the study was widespread among subjects.

Several of those interviewed from the "returned" group had done both undergraduate and graduate study in the United States. Only two undergraduates and four graduate students had studied for only one year. Twelve had studied three years or more in the United States. Financing was varied; most undergraduates had been privately financed, while most graduates had received fellowships. The distribution of fields of study is shown in the tabulation. The distributions are similar to those given in Chapter 2 (Table 4) for students in the domestic study, although the categories are not identical.

	No.
Engineering (all branches)	7
Medicine and public health	3
Biological subjects	3
Business curriculums	2
Architecture	1
Library science	1
Various arts and humanities	9

Despite the limitations of the sample of returned students, numerous trends are apparent and on some topics there is virtual unanimity. Moreover, wherever tentative conclusions concern subjects dealt with in the domestic study, there is rather close congruence.

SETTING OF THE STUDY

Since the intensive interviews provide the core of the data for this monograph, the conclusions may be illuminated by a few general remarks about the settings in which they were obtained. The returned students were interviewed in Mexico City except for a few in Guadalajara, settings which were either the birthplace or had provided part of the pre-United States educational experience of most subjects in both studies. Guadalajara, second city of Mexico with around half a million population, is more conservative, more easygoing, more "typical" of Mexico, than is Mexico City. Nevertheless, it is a very modern city, where the influence of the United States is of longer standing and more marked than in, say, Puebla, its nearest counterpart among Mexican cities.

Mexico City is one of the larger cities in the hemisphere in population and is cosmopolitan in character. In many ways it is an international city, but it is also the major focus of the political, cultural, and economic life of the nation. Physically and culturally it blends European and United States influences into a distinctively Mexican pattern. Here center the arts, the publishing business, industry, and the government. There are slums, modern Paris-like boulevards, narrow streets from colonial times, skyscrapers, United States–like suburbs and traffic problems. The energetic and competitive pace of life, especially among the middle and upper classes, contradicts all popular stereotypes of Latin America.

Los Angeles approaches Mexico City in population and is the center of a substantially larger metropolitan area. It offers the usual urban facilities. Cultural and recreational facilities are extensive, but they are so dispersed and public transportation is so lacking that they are difficult of access to most Mexican students. Except for a few excursions, most Mexican students do not travel far from the University, although they may live some distance from it. This is true of students at all the Los Angeles institutions.

The University of California's Los Angeles campus is in the western part of the city, a relatively new and expensive middle- to upper-class residential section. The university maintains few housing facilities and all students have difficulty living near campus; only about 30 per cent live within two miles. The major housing problems for Mexican students are financial. There is some residential discrimination, but Mexican students may never personally see or encounter any overt discrimination against themselves or others.

The university charges tuition fees to out-of-state residents which may be remitted for outstanding graduate students. Of all California high school graduates only about 20 per cent can meet admission requirements; somewhat higher standards are used in considering out-of-state applications. At the time of the study the enrollment exceeded 13,300. About two thirds of the students are male and about one quarter are in the graduate school. Because of the extensive junior college system in California, the number of new students entering with advanced standing is normally greater than the number entering as freshmen.

The lack of residential facilities at UCLA contributes to the relatively low development of the campus community and aggravates the impersonality of the metropolitan location. Student services are well developed as a result of an effort to alleviate some aspects of this problem and there is a separate and well-organized Foreign Student Adviser's Office, with a staff of several people under the direction of an assistant dean who has had considerable experience in Latin America. Special courses in English for foreigners are offered and students with linguistic difficulties are limited in the number of courses they may take. Two student clubs, International House (a group working toward the establishment of a residence center) and the Cosmos Club, as well as various off-campus organizations, give special attention to foreign students.

Despite favorable attitudes toward foreign students among both administrative officers and students, the foreign student attracts little attention. The presence of some 520 foreign students (including about 175 on quota-immigrant visas) and substantial numbers from Negro, Japanese-American, and other domestic ethnic groups gives a cosmopolitan air to the campus. Although individual members of particular ethnic groups may achieve recognition — a Negro has been student body president, a Japanese has been yell leader, a Pakistani has twice headed the student delegation to the model United Nations, the student paper publishes occasional interviews with foreign students — most foreign students are taken for granted by both students and faculty. With Mexico less than 150 miles away and with nearly half a million Mexican-Americans resident in the county, the Mexican student especially has little exotic quality upon which he can capitalize. Save for a few special groups and the Foreign Student Adviser's Office, the Mexican student finds himself in a friendly but impersonal atmosphere. Nevertheless, except for the difficulty of establishing social relationships, the university setting seems congenial to most Mexican students.

THE WRITTEN INSTRUMENTS

The use of written instruments was undertaken primarily on an experimental basis. Although the instruments used varied in productiveness, the experiments suggest that properly prepared instruments can be used in cross-cultural studies of this type. Despite the limitations of our sample and the lack of pre-testing of our instruments, some instruments gave results we considered reliable or at the least tending to confirm our interview materials. Full details and copies of the instruments presumably would be of interest only to the specialist and are not included here.

Background Data. Each student supplying data, whether from interviews or in writing, filled out a lengthy background data sheet. Sheets were not always completed but all gave substantial information about personal history, family relationships, educational background of subject and other family members, occupation, and similar data. In most cases data were sufficient to make reliable class identifications if upper-middle- and upper-class groupings are merged.

Information about America Test. This test was adapted from one prepared at the University of Pennsylvania for use with Indian students. It attempted to discriminate between knowledge one might get from books or other sources at a distance, and knowledge one could only get through residence and informal sources. An adapted form was used with Japanese students at Ohio State University. In a preliminary test administration with a few Mexican and American students, scores of the two groups were very similar, supporting the view that Mexican students are better prepared for American life than are Indian and Japanese students. As both Mexican and American students were irritated by the test, it was abandoned as not sufficiently productive.

Such trends as were suggested in the preliminary testing were harmonious with data from other sources. Mexican students tended to idealize the United States more than American students did. They tended to score noticeably lower than American students on knowledge of slang, on a few formal social adjustment questions, and in identifying prominent United States citizens in business and politics. They tended to score slightly higher than American students in identifying musicians, writers, and movie and TV personalities. Except for use in comparing student groups it seems unlikely that any test of information about the United States will be very useful for Mexican students.

Sentence Completion Test. A modification of the Sachs Sentence Completion Test was administered to forty-two Mexican students. The initial modification was developed by John Bennett and his associates for use with Japanese students at Ohio State University. To permit maximum comparability, practically no change was made in the Ohio State modification except to introduce one additional category specially applicable to Mexican students.

The test was translated into Spanish. Answers were written in Spanish and the test was scored by judges with a knowledge of Spanish. Scoring was on the manifest content level rather than on the analytic level. In the test the incomplete sentences are randomly ordered. For scoring they were grouped in the categories shown in Appendix Table 1.

In order to ascertain the areas in which significant differences exist within the Mexican student group the ten students with lowest total scores and the ten with highest total scores were compared. We assumed that the lowest scorers are the best adjusted and the highest scorers the poorest adjusted. This segregation was made on the basis of the subtotal of the fifteen categories believed to be most reliable. Mean scores for each category were calculated for both groups and the significance of the intergroup differences between these mean scores was then tested. The statistical results are shown in Appendix Table 1; interpretation was given in Chapter 2.

Appendix Table 1. Comparison of the Mean Scores on the Sentence Completion Test of the Ten Highest Scorers and the Ten Lowest Scorers in General Adjustment

Category	t values
I. Attitude toward friends and acquaintances....	.86
II. Attitudes toward supervisors at work or school	1.97
III. Attitudes toward people supervised..........	5.51**
IV. Attitudes toward colleagues at work or school	1.61
V. Fears	.90
VI. Guilt feelings.............................	.58
VII. Attitude toward own abilities...............	3.14**
VIII. Attitude toward past......................	3.09**
IX. Attitude toward future....................	2.28*
X. Goals	4.59**
XI. Self-awareness and acceptance.............	3.23**
XII. Perception of social roles.................	2.13*
XIII. Perception of and expectation of personality changes	1.28
XIV. Family adjustment	2.68*
XV. Occupational adjustment..................	2.69*

* Significant at the .05 level (.05 = 2.101).
** Significant at the .01 level (.01 = 2.878).

In our opinion the sentence completion type of instrument is productive with Mexican students, especially when administered in Spanish. In retrospect we feel that several categories in the original Sachs test as reported in Abt and Bellack * that we omitted would have been more useful than some of the new categories introduced by Bennett and ourselves. Our only caution is that any analytic interpretation of the responses should be done only by persons thoroughly familiar with Mexican culture. For example, when a Mexican male says he can remember no serious conflicts with his mother, he probably is reporting reality and not repress-

* Lawrence Edwin Abt and Leopold Bellak, editors, *Projective Psychology: Clinical Approaches to the Total Personality* (New York: Knopf, 1950).

ing; the chances are that his mother neither disciplined him nor denied him anything in his life.

American Ideology and Popular Beliefs Test. A written test concerning American ideology and popular beliefs was filled out by thirty-eight Mexican students and proved very useful. The students were given ninety-four brief statements believed to be conspicuous in American ideology and beliefs or in foreign students' ideas about America. The statements were mostly identical with those employed in a test developed at Ohio State University for Japanese students. More substitutions or additions might have made the test more relevant for Mexican students, but in the interests of comparability we preferred to make as little change as possible.

On the right of each statement were six boxes in which the student registered with an X whether he (a) personally agreed or disagreed with the statement; (b) thought the majority of Mexicans would agree or disagree with the statement; and (c) thought the majority of Americans would agree or disagree with the statement. Initially, the test was administered twice with the students asked to give their estimate of American agreement or disagreement separately. Because of resistances to the time involved, we reluctantly combined the two, but a comparison of scores for the two methods indicates that the halo effect was slight and there is no significant difference in the medians or ranges for the two conditions of administration.

The test statements were arranged in random order. For scoring they were then grouped into categories formulated at Ohio State University after a study of raw scores and the application of simple tests for significance. The categories used are listed in Appendix Table 2.

As a check, the instrument was administered to eighty-one upper division and graduate students in a course in culture and personality at UCLA. It was also administered to forty-nine students in anthropology courses at Los Angeles City College. Differences in background probably accounted for the substantial difference in mean scores of the two groups. Consequently they were not combined, and wherever an "American norm" was desired, the results from UCLA students were used on the grounds that the UCLA students more closely resembled the Mexican students in the type of institution they were attending and in their scholastic level. These students were also asked to judge whether they thought the majority of Mexicans would agree or disagree with each item.

Scoring each column of the tests provided measures of the following: personal ideologies of Mexican students, Mexican estimates of American ideology, Mexican estimates of Mexican ideology, personal ideologies of American students, American estimates of American ideology, and American estimates of Mexican ideology. Two methods of scoring were used. One gave a relationship score by which it was possible to rank each student as to the degree to which his personal ideology agreed or disagreed with his estimates of Mexican and American ideology and the degree

Appendix Table 2. Comparison of Mexican and American Ideologies

Questionnaire Category	Student Ideologies Are More Alike Than:				Mexican Student Ideology Is More Like:	
	Either Is with Estimate of Own National Ideology	Americans Are with Own Estimate of American Ideology ‡	Mexicans Are with Own Estimate of Mexican Ideology	Either Is with Own Estimate of American Ideology	American Estimate of American Ideology Than Like Mexican Ideology	Mexican Estimate of American Ideology Than Like Mexican Ideology
	Section A					
I. Attitudes toward America *†		X		X		
IIA. Attitudes toward large concentrations of power in both government and business *†		X			X	X
IIB. Attitudes toward individual freedom as it relates to government regulation *†	X	X	X		(equal)	X
IIC. Faith in the integrity of government and government officials *		X			X	X
III. Belief in the importance of knowledge as an instrument of human welfare *	X	X	X		X	X
IVA. Social equality of women *		X	X		X	X
IVB. Loyalty to parents versus loyalty to mate			X		X	X
V. Status concern *†	X	X	X	X	X	X
VI. Ethical behavior *†	X	X	X	X	X	X
	Section B					
A. Attitudes toward children *	X	X	X	X	X	X
B. Individual behavior †		X		X		X
C. Social outlook *		X		X		

* Mexican student ideology is more like Mexican estimate of American ideology than American student ideology is like American estimate of American ideology.

† American student ideology is more like Mexican estimate of American ideology than like American estimate of American ideology.

‡ American student ideology agrees less with American estimate of American ideology than does Mexican student ideology.

to which his estimates of Mexican and American ideology were similar or different. The second was a simple computation of percentages of agreement for each statement which permitted group comparisons of personal ideologies and estimates of Mexican and American ideologies.

The relationships scores made it possible to rank-order individuals on those categories which formed continua. For example, in Category I, Attitudes toward America, individuals could be ranked along a continuum from America-best-nation to America-not-best. Individuals could also be rank-ordered in terms of agreement between personal ideologies, estimates of Mexican ideology, and estimates of American ideology.

The relationship measures probably would have been more useful if we had been able to secure more personality data on students. Actually they contributed little. No correlations were found, for example, between good adjustment as determined by the Sentence Completion Test and scores on ideologies tests. The five persons whose personal ideologies were closest to their estimate of Mexican ideologies also believed their personal ideologies close to their estimates of American ideologies, and hence saw little difference between the ideologies of the two nations. Similar relationships are not apparent for other students.

There were some interesting results when the percentage of agreement scores was figured. For both Mexican and American students, percentages of those who personally agreed with each item, and percentages of those who thought most Mexicans or Americans would agree with each item were calculated. Mean agreement scores for each category were then found. The difference between the means gave a measure of the extent to which personal ideologies differed from estimates of Mexican and American ideologies and of the difference between estimates of Mexican and American ideologies by Mexican and American students. More sophisticated statistical techniques seemed hardly justified in view of the preliminary nature of the instrument and the sampling inadequacies.

The most striking conclusion suggested by the methods used is the close similarity of the ideologies of Mexican and American students. The most important points are summarized in Appendix Table 2. These similarities are the more striking when it is realized that except in Category III (Belief in the importance of knowledge as an instrument of human welfare), and Category IVB (Loyalty to parents versus loyalty to mate), the personal ideologies of Mexican students are closer to the American students' estimates of the majority of Americans than are the American students themselves. Even in these two categories, the Mexican students are closer to their own estimate of American ideology than to their estimate of Mexican ideology.

For every category except III, Mexican and American student ideologies are more alike than either group is to its own estimate of its own national ideology. The evidence suggests, then, that Mexican and American students tend toward a common student ideology which for both groups is substantially different from their estimates of their own national ideologies.

In general, the American student tends to see more differences between American and Mexican ideologies than do Mexican students. Moreover, the American student tends to disagree more with his national ideology and in part — but only in part — to move toward Mexican ideology. The Mexican student, on the other hand, although he may disagree less with his own national ideology in most categories, tends strongly to move toward his estimate of American ideology, and in some cases, even closer to the American students' estimate of American ideology. The extent of this movement may be slightly, but only slightly, exaggerated by the wholehearted movement of the women students toward American ideology in the categories Social equality of women and Attitudes toward children. Hence, while still strongly rejecting the United States (as in Category I, Attitudes toward America), the Mexican student in some categories becomes more American than the Americans.

There are several possible explanations for this phenomenon. Undoubtedly the United States control sample is somewhat atypical. Mexican students may have been pre-selected for adaptability and acceptance of United States ideology. Politeness also may have had some influence on the results (although some of the respondents were far from polite about the United States and the questionnaire). Nevertheless, we believe the results at least partly reflect changes in the attitudes and ideologies of the students since coming to the United States.

DISCUSSION BY CATEGORIES

I. Attitudes toward America. (Sample statement: The American people have more initiative, ambition, and ability than the people of other countries.)

Mexican and American students agree closely in their estimate of American ideology. However, Mexican students estimate that many more Mexicans would accept the statements under this category than do the American students. A striking difference occurs in the personal ideologies, for on every item, a larger percentage of Mexican students than UCLA students agrees with the item. Thus 47 per cent of the Mexican students agree that the American pattern of institutions is best and will work anywhere, while only 5 per cent of the American students agree. Similarly, 30 per cent of the Mexican students agree that "The United States government never breaks a treaty or goes back on its word in international relations" as opposed to only 1 per cent of American students, while 41 per cent of the Mexican students agree that world peace will be best preserved if the United States is the strongest nation militarily as opposed to only 17 per cent of UCLA students.

Seventy-six per cent of the Mexicans and 77 per cent of the UCLA students agree that the majority of Americans believe the white race to be superior to others, but only 2 per cent of UCLA students (and 0 per cent of LACC students) believe this personally in contrast to 5 per cent of the Mexican students.

IIA. Attitudes toward large concentrations of power in both government and business. (Sample statement: Free competition is the basic principle of sound business enterprise.)

Mexican and American students disagree more on this subject than on most. American students are mildly in favor of big government and government spending, are about equally divided about the merits of free enterprise, and are distinctly doubtful that the activities of capitalists are for the good of the public (only 20 per cent agree). Except for government spending, many more Mexicans accept statements in this category, reaching 91 per cent agreement that free competition is the basic principle of sound business enterprise. Mexican and American students tend to agree on their estimate of the opinions of most Americans, but Mexican students consider that Mexican ideology is much closer to American ideology in this area than is the case with American students.

IIB. Attitudes toward individual freedom as it relates to government regulation. (Sample statement: People should be permitted complete freedom to practice whatever religion they choose.)

The opinions of Mexican and American students tend to agree more than do their estimates of American ideology but interesting contradictions occur. Both groups agree strongly that academic freedom is necessary but only 60 per cent of the American students, as opposed to 89 per cent of the Mexicans, think that a majority of Americans would support this view. Both groups agree equally (92 per cent) that people should be free to create and join any kind of political party they wish but again 82 per cent of the Mexicans consider that the majority of Americans would agree against only 46 per cent of the American students. Confusingly, however, in view of the strong endorsement by both groups of several statements, 62 per cent of the Mexicans and 23 per cent of the American students consider censorship necessary for the maintenance of moral and social order, while 38 per cent of the Mexican students and 32 per cent of the American students think a dictator is sometimes a good thing. Moreover, 29 per cent of American students think that the majority of Americans would agree with them (but only 11 per cent of Mexican students think the same). For both groups of students then there are ambivalences toward authority, ambivalences we have already noted for the Mexican students in the Sentence Completion Test.

IIC. Faith in the integrity of government and government officials. (Sample statement: The government should be respected because they know best.)

Mexican and American students here differ more in personal opinions than in their estimate of American ideology. However, only 9 per cent of the Mexican students think that a majority of Americans would consider government the source of all corruption and graft, as compared to 37 per cent of the American students. The Mexican scores again show some ambivalence and much more distrust of government than is the case with American students. Thirty-seven per cent of Mexican students and only 4 per cent of American students think that government should be trusted, but 56 per cent of Mexicans think politicians should not be trusted, and 62 per cent think government cannot be as efficient as private business as opposed to 37 and 36 per cent respectively for American students.

III. Belief in the importance of knowledge (especially scientific knowledge) as an instrument of human welfare. (Sample statement: It is not knowledge but faith that we need to solve our most serious problems.)

Mexican and American student estimates of American ideology are very similar. However, more Mexican students than American students express belief in the importance of knowledge; the difference is especially marked with respect to the relative value of education. Again some ambivalences are suggested, for slightly more Mexican students than American believe that faith is more important than knowledge in solving serious problems and that scientific discoveries need to be controlled.

IVA. Social equality of women. (Sample statement: Husband and wife are partners and should cooperate together on all decisions.)

On every item Mexican students think the majority of Americans accord more equality to women than American students do, but both think the majority of Mexicans would accord much less equality to women than would the majority of Americans. Mexican students as a group agree more with their estimate of the attitude of the majority of Americans than with their estimate of Mexican ideology. However, it should be noted that acceptance is highest among women students and that a few Mexican men strongly disbelieve in social equality for women. Furthermore, as a group, American students agree more that women should have social equality than Mexican students do.

IVB. Loyalty to parents versus loyalty to mate. (Sample statement: One's first duty is to parents, even after marriage.)

The Mexican students' estimate of American ideology is close to that of the American students. Mexican students' personal opinions differ markedly from their estimate of the majority of Mexicans in favor of primary loyalty to the mate. Nevertheless, many more Mexicans than Americans still put loyalty to parents ahead of loyalty to mate. The one unexpected exception is that apparently slightly more American students than Mexicans approve of parental interference with mate choices.

V. Status concern. (Sample statement: Each person should know his proper place in society.)

Mexican and American students agree fairly closely in their estimates of both Mexican and American ideology except on the question of discrimination, where 68 per cent of American students feel that the majority of Americans are opposed to discrimination, an opinion shared by only 44 per cent of Mexican students. However, in their personal ideologies, except for almost complete rejection of discrimination by both groups, Mexican students are much more concerned with status than American students are. For example, 77 per cent of the Mexican students believe a person should know his proper place in society as compared with only 30 per cent of the UCLA students. Students at LACC are much more concerned with status than are UCLA students, and approach the Mexican score.

VI. Ethical behavior. (Sample statement: If one doesn't watch out for his own interests, others will take advantage of him.)

On matters of conscience and principles, there is little difference between the personal ideologies of Mexican and American students, but substantially more Mexicans than Americans believe that it is proper to do anything that is legal and that unless one looks after his own interests, people will take advantage of him. On the whole, American students consider the majority of Mexicans to be more ethical than the Mexican students do, while the Mexican students consider Americans as a whole to be more ethical in ideology than the American students do. Moreover, both groups give themselves better scores than they do their compatriots.

A. Attitudes toward children. (Sample statement: The best way to raise children is to make them do as they are told.)

In general, American students consider the majority of Americans to be less permissive toward children than Mexicans do. However, both in their personal ideologies and in their estimate of American ideologies, American students consider children much more important to family life than the Mexicans think they do. Mexican students see themselves as much less strict in their attitudes toward children than the majority of Mexicans; but they still tend to be significantly more strict than the American students.

B. Individual behavior. (Sample statement: Most rich people are really quite unhappy; happiness does not always accompany success.)

Differences between American and Mexican students' estimates of American ideology probably are not significant. On most items, the personal ideology scores are also somewhat similar. In general, the American students are less concerned with money than the Mexicans think most Americans are; in fact, while differences probably are not significant, the Mexican students show a slight tendency toward greater concern with money values than the American students do. The greatest discrepancy between the Mexican students' estimate of American ideology and American student ideology is in relation to time; only 14 per cent of the Mexican students think that a majority of Americans would agree that it is "wasteful to be in a hurry all the time." In contrast, 37 per cent of the American students think the majority of Americans would agree and 70 per cent of the American students agree personally (as compared with 83 per cent of Mexican students).

C. Social outlook. (Sample statement: The larger the business, the greater the profits in the hands of the few.)

On most items in this category, Mexican and American students' personal ideologies and estimates of the ideology of the majority of Americans show insignificant differences. On two items differences are marked. Sixty-one per cent of Mexicans believe that "Liberty and equalitarianism guarantee that the United States is a nation without social classes," a statement subscribed to by only .04 per cent of American students. Similarly, 70 per cent of the Mexican students believe women to be less practical than men as opposed to only 25 per cent of the American students. While trends are slight, Mexican students appear to have somewhat more confidence in business, to include a larger percentage of very conservative persons (13 per cent of Mexicans to .01 per cent of Americans agree that "What worked in the past is good enough for the present") and slightly larger percentage who agree uncritically that "any change is for the good" (17 per cent of Mexicans to .04 per cent of Americans).

TRADITIONAL VALUES

Both student opinion and the analyses of the investigators emphasize the radical changes occurring in Mexican value systems and ideologies. It further appears that the students as a whole are changing faster than the Mexican population is. To check these assumptions a further analysis of the Ideologies and Popular Beliefs questionnaire was undertaken.

As many items as seemed relevant were reclassified in terms of the acceptance or rejection of traditional values. This involved an estimate by Beals of the meaning of each statement and the result can be no better than the accuracy of that estimate. The items used were grouped into a series of categories given in Appendix Table 3.

In this table we show the variation by categories of the mean differences between the students' personal ideologies and their estimates of the ideology held by most Mexicans, rather than simple agreement or disagreement with the traditional values items. This was done to compensate for possible biases or inaccuracies in the identification of items as representing traditional values. Hence it is perhaps more accurate to describe Appendix Table 3 as showing the extent to which Mexican students' personal beliefs vary from their judgments regarding Mexican ideology in a direction we believe to be away from traditional values.

The results are generally confirmatory of other evidence. Differences between the personal ideologies of the students and their estimates of Mexican tradition suggest that students approve of greater freedom for women (undoubtedly colored by the relatively large number of women in the sample) and more permissive child-rearing practices, have much greater faith in reason, show less religious conformity, and have greater faith in government and politics. Differences of personal ideologies from the Mexican estimate are appreciably smaller in relation to belief in education, confidence in free enterprise and individual initiative, acceptance of authority, and in equalitarianism and tolerance. Examination of crude scores, however, suggests that the smaller difference here does not mean the Mexican student is more traditional but that in these categories he believes most Mexicans also to be relatively untraditional. They differ scarcely at all from their countrymen in the importance they attach to kin and parents, in their adherence to spiritual and humanistic values, and in their attitudes toward the United States. Moreover, in all three, crude scores suggest the students see not only themselves but the majority of Mexicans as very strongly traditional in outlook.

Appendix Table 3. Mean Difference between Students' Personal Ideologies and Their Estimate of the Ideologies of the Majority of Mexicans in Selected Categories Arranged in Rank Order from Greatest Difference (Least Traditional) to Least Difference (Most Traditional)*

Category	Mean Difference
Position of women........................	21.84
Child-rearing practices......................	16.30
Faith in reason...........................	13.95
Religion	13.87
Faith in government and politicians...........	12.58
Belief in free enterprise and individual initiative..	7.26†
Importance of education and knowledge........	6.63†
Importance of kin and parents................	5.61
Acceptance of authority.....................	4.79†
Equalitarianism	3.37†
Adherence to spiritual and humanistic values.....	1.30
Attitudes toward the United States.............	.97

* N = 38. Because of scoring methods employed, the maximum difference theoretically possible would be 50, the minimum, 0.

† But the majority of Mexicans were also estimated to be relatively untraditional.

A few other observations may be of interest. Twenty-one students saw themselves as more conservative than their estimate of the majority of Mexicans in one or more categories, excluding Attitudes toward America. (In numerous categories, individual students often agreed with their Mexican estimate.) Ten of these considered themselves more conservative in only one category, eight in two categories, two in three categories, and one in four categories.

In the category Atttiudes toward America, the majority of the students agreed with their generally unfavorable Mexican estimate. Nine were in some degree less favorable than their Mexican estimate and only six were more favorable. In other categories, the following numbers saw themselves as more traditional than their Mexican estimate:

	No.
Position of women	0
Child-rearing practices	1
Faith in reason	1
Religion	3
Faith in government and politicians	1
Belief in free enterprise and individual initiative	6
Importance of education and knowledge	2
Importance of kin and parents	4
Acceptance of authority	6
Equalitarianism and tolerance	7
Adherence to spiritual and humanistic values	6

The results confirm the data from interviews and show striking similarity to categories of change listed by Humphrey. Unfortunately, two interpretations seem possible. The first is that the returned student retains and exhibits the greatest effects of his sojourn in the United States in those categories of behavior and ideas wherein he experienced the greatest change while in the United States. Alternatively, it may be that those Mexicans who already are least traditional in these categories are those who come to the United States.

Index

Acculturation: theoretical and methodological problems of, 4–6, 110; student role in Mexican, 5–6, 109–15 *passim*; characteristics of Mexican, 6; 110–11; Social Science Research Council seminar in, 110; student as agent, 111–14 *passim*

Adjustment: problems of personal and social, 4, 7, 33–34, 72–73; cultural factors involved, 7, 43, 66; of Mexican students in United States, 41–44, 47, 57, 59–64 *passim,* 131; suggestions for handling difficulties in, 119–20

Agrarian revolutionists. *See* Revolution, Mexican

Agricultural sciences, holders of fellowships in, 67

Agringado, term of opprobrium, 103

America. *See* United States

American High School in Mexico, 30, 37, 46

American Ideologies and Popular Beliefs Test: results of, 44–47, 134–39; administration of, 132; American control group used, 132; description, 132; scoring, 132–34; Mexican and American groups compared, 133; traditional values derived from ideologies, 139–41

American students, characterized by Mexicans, 62, 77, 79

American universities: student opinions and attitudes concerning, 31–32, 74–84; prior advanced study by Mexican students in, 38; selection of by Mexican students, 39–40; experiences of students in, 66–72; reasons for failures in, 67–68; lack of preparation for grading systems in, 68, 75; academic ac-

complishments in, 69–72; compared with Mexican, 79, 80; difficulties with examinations in, 80; criticisms of by returnees, 108–9; need of explanation of system, 118; bureaucratic failures in, 118; importance of alternative academic goals, 118. *See also* UCLA

Americans: prior contacts with, 39; as source of preconceptions, 50

Anti-Americanism: nature of, 8, 47–49; not applied to individuals, 8, 49; sources of, 48–49; modifications of among students, 49, 50; explanations of, 52–53, 103–5 *passim*; function of among returnees, 113; mentioned, 94

Anti-clericalism in Mexico, 13, 111. *See also* Religion

Army, Mexican, as political force, 13

Art, Mexican, as social force, 25–26

Authoritarianism: influence on interpersonal relationships, 22, 42; in Mexican teaching methods, 29

Automobiles, lack of felt, 63

Bachillerato. See Degrees

Buddhists, 27

Bureaucracy: growth of Mexican, 12; general criticisms of, 57, 76; in universities, 76

Business: American, in Mexico, 48, 95, 108; general attitudes toward, 136, 139; in United States, 87–88, 95; problems of returnees in business, 103

Businessmen: American colony in Mexico criticized, 107

Camacho, Avila, election begins industrialization period, 11

142